LIKE NIGHT AND DAY
A Look at Chicago Baseball, 1964-1969

By John M. O'Donnell

ISBN: 1-4196-9055-8

ISBN-13: 9781419690556

Visit www.booksurge.com to order additional copies.

Acknowledgements

The author would like to thank his mom, who took him to his first Cub game and his dad, who took him to his first White Sox game. Sincere thanks extended to Tim White, for his expertise and insight. Special thanks to wife Betsy, sons Brian & Michael, daughters Julie & Katie, brothers Mark & Denny, sister Jeanne, brother-in-law Ken and niece Colleen for their endless support and tolerance of my baseball addiction. And to the friends along the way who told me to hang in there—especially Frank, Chris, and Greg—thank you.

Preface

June 30, 1964 and July 4, 1964. I know I'm more likely to forget the dates of my kids' birthdays, our wedding anniversary, or even my birthday before I forget these two dates of my first Cub game and White Sox game.

Why the passion? In spite of all the strikes, lockouts, scandals, etc., why do we keep coming back? It seems that the fan is much more loyal to the industry than the industry is to the fan. I doubt if there's an all-encompassing answer, but I do know this: the game of baseball is bigger than its problems. It has to be in order to survive through it all.

So if you're someone who reads baseball stuff in the winter time, if you're someone who determines the probable starting pitchers days before attending a game, if you're someone who once or twice kept score *at home*, then this little book is for you. If you've never done those things, don't worry, there's still time.

As you travel east bound on Addison Street from Western Avenue, you'll notice houses separated by only a few feet. I grew up in a Chicago neighborhood not unlike this one. For worse or better (fortunately, better for us), you know your neighbors. You can smell what they're having for supper, you can hear which of the *four* TV stations they have on (remember, this is mid 1960's), and you can eavesdrop on some interesting conversations. It might take eight minutes to mow the front "yard", and another seven to do the back. Front porches with a swing invite friendly chatter. Anonymity in this environment is not going to happen. This is the kind of neighborhood you find around Wrigley Field.

The red sign. You know the one I'm talking about. I know it has a fancy name, but you know immediately where you are once you see this red sign. It tells you that this is "Home of Chicago Cubs." It's also been home to the football Bears, and for a short while the soccer Sting, but the chief resident at Clark and Addison has been a baseball team. Back in 1964, the red sign also told you what visiting team was in town, and for how long. In my first grade mindset, different teams meant different things. "San Francisco" meant sluggers: Mays, McCovey, Cepeda, Hart, etc., so let's hope the wind is blowing in. "New York" meant that the Cubs might win. And "Cincinnati", the opponent on June 30, presented such a fascinating conglomeration of "C's", "i's", and "n's" that I didn't even think too much about the ball club. How many common words are there that look anything like "Cincinnati"? (Maybe cinnamon, but that's a stretch).

You can't talk about Cincinnati without talking about their logo: an old-time baseball player with a big baseball for his head. Baseball logos were great, and some still are, and this one with the big baseball head was near the top of the list. Another bonus: their nickname back then was a syllable longer back then and a notch cooler: the Redlegs. We weren't just going to see the Reds; we're going to watch the Redlegs!

Ever since I was a kid, I remember public transportation being promoted by the Cub organization a lot more than the folks on the South side. I never really understood why until I started driving and tried to find a parking space. Back in 1964, parking on the street could be found within two blocks of the ballpark. Now on a good day, it's close to a mile. Our first trek to Wrigley Field landed us a spot on a street named Eddy (I remember this well because it reminded me of an all-American running back at Notre Dame at the time called Nick Eddy). In spite of being so close to the ballpark, we still managed to get turned around and lost for a few minutes after the game.

Walking to the northeast corner of Clark & Addison is an experience in sensory overload. Your eyes are focused on the aforementioned red sign, but your ears pick up something else. The cops' whistles as they direct traffic has been embedded in my memory. If you've been there you'll remember the cadence: one longer note followed by two very short ones. I took note as to how the officers directed the flow of cars and pedestrians in a commanding yet not overbearing way. The pace was quite brisk, but not too brisk for me. After all, this was my first game.

Tickets are purchased on the day of the game. Scalpers? Not with ten thousand people attending. Cost? General admission, commonly referred to as grandstand, would set adults back a dollar or so, with kids even less. My mom would take me on Ladies' Day to conserve on the family budget. (I seldom saw the Cubs lose on Ladies' Day. Perhaps the team had a little added incentive. Ironically, an early loss occurred when we thought we were attending a Ladies' Day game, only to find out that it was Senior Citizens' Day. When did these days become extinct?)

Purchasing tickets in advance for our family was not common. P.K. Wrigley and the O'Donnell household believed in spontaneity. Wrigley's policy held thousands of tickets, every day, for walk-up sales. As a kid I wondered who would want to buy a ticket in advance? You didn't know who would be pitching (if it was way in advance), you wouldn't know if it would rain, you wouldn't know if you'd have a make-up Little League game rescheduled that day, and you wouldn't know if you'd be grounded. Besides, by buying a grandstand ticket, you had your choice of any seat above the box seats. You could even sit in the upper deck, if it was open.

Bombardment of the senses continued on the other side of the turnstiles. The dominating aroma belonged to the smoky links. Smells incredible, but I'm too excited to eat. The predominant sound was that of vendors hawking scorecards through rich, husky voices: "Lineups, lineups." Not much else was said by these gentlemen whose median age appeared to be ninety-seven. The scorecards that vendors pushed and we bought were a treasure back then, and deserve a closer look later. Creative work, to say the least. But what really caught my eye in the concourse were pictures of the ballplayers. This might have been my first game, but who wouldn't stop to stare at photos of Ron Santo, Billy Williams, or Ernie Banks? I remember seeing these photos extend for quite a distance right above the concession stand, and I also recall these images being in place for a number of years. It seems to suggest, looking back, a more stable time when the turnover of players was not as common. If it was, would management go through the hassle of putting up new pictures all the time?

Then it happens. All the preliminaries are over and it's time to get serious. You climb the stairs and see the inside of Wrigley Field for the first time. A genuine "wow" experience. Some perspective is needed here–remember that black and white televisions and telecasts were the rule back then. And remember, too, the size of the yard in your typical two-flat Chicago west side home. So I had absolutely no frame of reference for what I was about to see. Never had I see grass so green, so expansive, so manicured. There are some firsts one will always remember: your first kiss, birth of your first child, your first successful heart transplant, and the first time you ever set eyes on a major league baseball field.

Would having a color TV set make a difference? Sure. Seeing everything in shades of gray doesn't prepare you for the red in the Cincinnati uniform, the green on the outfield ivy, or the blue of the Cub hat and pinstripes. (As a kid I wondered that if they're called cubs, shouldn't they be brown instead of blue? Five years later I got an answer to that question when the San Diego Padres made their debut with brown and yellow uniforms. Not a pretty sight).

Gawking at this field makes you oblivious of all else. Sensory overload kicks in again; there's just too much green at once. (There's still a tinge of that when I attend a game now; a sense of awe at something I consider a natural masterpiece.) My mom finally breaks me out of this trance by leading us to our seats. I start to wonder that if things are this good now, what's it like when the game starts? Unfortunately, my 40-plus years of attending have taught me that the pre-game experience is often as good as the day gets.

Something finally takes my attention away from the field. That would be a 75 foot-long magnet known as the center field scoreboard. Back in the days before expansion, before there were some 295 teams or so, there was this scoreboard. This green-gray monstrosity about three stories in height comfortably accommodated all teams in both leagues. On a weekday, which is when Ladies' Day fell, the words "Nite Game" spread across the board in creative fashion. Sometimes it showed in straight horizontal lettering, sometimes in diagonal configurations, and sometimes the words "no game" would appear if a couple of teams happened to be traveling. The Cubs and their opposition were situated in the middle left-hand side of the scoreboard. Rust-colored horizontal lines highlighted the game you were watching. For the second time I got to marvel at the spelling of "Cincinnati"; this time the letters were legibly squished together so that there would be no intrusion into the box reserved for the first inning. Even more impressive was how the operators managed to squeeze in "Philadelphia" or "San Francisco."

The right side of the board listed the American League match-ups. Directly across from the "Cubs" position on the center right side of the board was the word "Sox." They were always listed on top, because if the Cubs were at Wrigley Field, the Sox had to be the visitors batting first. It's not uncommon today to have both clubs home simultaneously, but in '64 it was very rare. In recent years, memory doesn't tell me just when, the South Siders went through a change in identity. On the scoreboard they became identified as "Chicago" instead of "Sox." More polite, more formal, more distant. From what I learned in Spanish class, this would be like referring to someone as "Usted" after calling them "tu" for many seasons.

The middle of the scoreboard tells you who is batting, the number of outs, and the count. This is the only baseball part of the scoreboard handled electronically (years later, electronic messages were relayed underneath the scoreboard. This entertainment center presents Cub trivia, pizza races, and other vital information). A point here needs to be made about this scoreboard's efficiency. Visiting fifteen major league ballparks, I've yet to see any ballpark come close to matching the swiftness with which the ball and strike count is given at Wrigley Field. It's almost like the scoreboard operator has ESP (without the N). Next time you're watching a game at Wrigley Field, see if you can detect the change in balls or strikes once the home plate umpire has made his decision. On a good day, I might catch the change once or twice. With such quick reflexes, I wonder if the Cubs' organization would be better served if the operator and the third basemen switch places.

In the 60's, the Cub telecasts would occasionally give air time to this magnificent scoreboard. When Don Kessinger (number 11) would bat with one out and a one ball, one strike count, Jack Brickhouse would inevitably mention that "aces are wild." At the ballpark I still notice these quirks, but I can't imagine that the savvy and sophisticated broadcasters and fans would acknowledge such things.

Toward the bottom of scoreboard central, the hits for each team appear in yellow. This, too, is manually operated, and looks like this: "VIS ___ HITS ___ CUBS." Why it's ordered this way is baffling and unorthodox, but it works.

Near the top of scoreboard central, in tiny numbers, are the umpires for today's ballgame. Scorecards feature the umpires' names with the corresponding numbers, if you really want to know. I wonder how many people purchase a scorecard, then notice the numbers on the scoreboard, then realize that the scorecard has the code for these umps, and then take the time to synthesize all this information. Seems like a lot of work–I maybe have done it thrice in over two hundred games.

A most attractive feature of this scoreboard for a first-grader is arithmetic application. It's not so much fun when the Cubs are getting pounded, but when the Cubs are ahead it's most enjoyable to add up the run total and calculate the difference between the Cubs and their opponent. The value *and* the color of the scoreboard numerals were significant; yellow meant that the team has scored and is still batting, and white means that the half-inning is over. Upon completion of the game, all numbers from the scoreboard are removed and replaced by two under the 10th inning. This means game over, the two numbers are the final score, and you can stop with the arithmetic.

In recent years, the pennants come down after the game and are replaced by a white flag with a large blue "W" or a large blue "L". I remember reading in recent years how Wrigley Field flags and pennants are used and abused by the elements. I also recall that the person in charge of flag maintenance and inventory sadly revealed the "L" flag is more frequently replaced than the "W" flag. In the words of Jack Brickhouse, "ouch."

The center field scoreboard at Wrigley Field is a masterpiece. It's ominous but not obnoxious, interactive but not intrusive, pleasant and not too commercial. It's made for Wrigley Field, but I could also see it in a few other places: the Art Institute, the Sistine Chapel, or my bedroom.

During batting practice, I was in complete awe of the distance that baseballs traveled. Being inexperienced, it seemed that every ball hit in the air may reach the clock perched atop the aforementioned scoreboard. Drives that I thought would land on Mars settled into an *infielder's* glove. It never occurred to me to watch the fielder calmly camping under a pop fly. Besides, keeping your focus on the flight of the ball was more fun. You just didn't see many drives like this hit in the back alley in a game of fast-pitchin' or back-yard whiffle ball.

Once the game began, I noticed a glaring omission: no play-by-play announcer. Where was Jack Brickhouse describing all these "headlines as they're being made?" It was a weird feeling. Jack's voice cued me in as to when to get excited; the commercials cued me in as to when to go to the bathroom (unless it featured the Hamm's bear, then I'd postpone my business until the cartoonish bear "from the land of sky-blue water" did his thing). At the ballpark, I was on my own. I had to figure out when I needed to get excited.

Our seats for these Ladies' Day games were in the grandstand territory behind third base. Here my mom, my sister and a host of other females sat for free. They were fine seats (there's not a whole lot of bad ones at W.F.), but I would have been content to sit anywhere. The sturdy and gray poles in front of us were no big deal. In the days prior to Prior and luxury suites, your view of fly balls was not obscured in the sections behind box seats. Speaking of box seats, I did wonder after the game what it would be like to sit so close to the field you could hear players and managers yelling at umps. Nevertheless, I was okay where we sat; a few neck contortions around the pole are hardly an inconvenience.

But something seemed out-of-place and asymmetrical. My first-grade vision told me that the bases were not equally distanced. The distance between 1st and 2nd, and between 3rd and home was much longer than the distance from home to first, and from 2nd to 3rd. Getting to first base did not seem that difficult, but now I understood why the Cubs never stole second; it was just too far away (one year the stolen base leader was Kessinger with 9!). And should the Cubs should be fortunate enough to reach third base, home still seemed miles away. How was a player ever going to score?

The answer that day was simple: no one was going to score. In fact, nobody was going to threaten and hardly anybody was going to reach base. Zeroes plastered the scoreboard—hardly a challenge to my arithmetic skills—thanks to the splendid pitching of Larry Jackson for the Cubs and Joey Jay (what a cool name) for the Redlegs.

The game was a blur, lasting only one hour and forty minutes. Its brevity was due to less down time between innings (fewer commercials), many outs, and few hits. The Cub offense managed two hits, but this doubled the Reds' output. When one considers how infrequently perfect games have been tossed at the major league level—there was a grand total of zero in the 1970's—it's astonishing that I almost witnessed one in my very first game.

Hot day, clear sky, and one base runner for the Reds. Can't ask for much more than that. I bet you can come up with that one player to reach base. I *bet* you can. Larry Jackson yielded one hit to the man who collected more hits than anyone who ever played—Pete Rose. When Rose led off the seventh inning, Jackson had retired the first 18 batters. On a 1-0 count, Rose singled cleanly into center field. Jackson then promptly disposed of the next nine batters, and the near-perfect one-hit gem was his. Immortality could have been Jackson's had Rose co-operated. Mine, too, I suppose—how many people do you know saw a perfect game in their major league debut? But in retrospect a one-hitter is a pretty effective way to get a kid hooked on baseball. I wonder if my passion for the game would have been the same had the Reds blown out the Cubs. First impressions can be potent.

This first game was also an omen. In 1964, Pete Rose was in his second year at the major league level, having won Rookie-of-the-Year honors during the previous season. I can think of only one man, Mike Schmidt, who has caused me more grief as a Chicago baseball fan. (I remember the infamous time when Schmidt homered four times in a game, or when his homer was the deciding tally in the 23-22 game, which I attended with several college buddies). But Rose was forever on my black list that day, and my feelings for him deteriorated one day years later when he spiked Ernie Banks.

Getting back to the game on June 30, the Cub offense managed to scratch out a run in the sixth inning. A leadoff walk to the catcher, Dick Bertell, a sacrifice bunt by Jackson, and a two out RBI single by Jimmy Stewart (the shortstop, not the actor) was the difference. Only two players hit safely that day: Rose with one single and Stewart with two. It was a Wonderful Day thanks to Jimmy Stewart. Imagine what might have happened if Rose and Stewart called in sick, a double no-hitter?! Something else to consider is this: these pitching gems occurred in spite of the presence of three future Hall-of-Famers (Frank Robinson, Ernie Banks, and Billy Williams), and three others who easily could be in the Hall (Ron Santo, Vada Pinson, and Rose). Pretty impressive pitching at cozy Wrigley Field that day.

It's now time to play guess the attendance. How many fans do you think showed up for this game? I'll set the over/under mark at 10,000. If you took the over, pay up! 8,380 was the attendance. Today I think you'd find more people at the Cubby Bear Lounge across the street after the game. When I first saw the attendance figure for that game I was surprised but not shocked. The upper deck was closed to fans, much like sections of a restaurant are closed to customers at quitting time. The low attendance figure was not just a Cub thing, either. Inspecting box scores from that era, four digit attendance numbers were not uncommon.

Any thoughts or comments on the drastic change in attendance over the years? I've got a couple. I think on one hand society has changed (I hesitate to use the word "evolved") from playing to spectating. Watching baseball is now a business more than a pass time. Something lost, something gained. The opportunity to watch highlights from any game is available every evening. In the 60's, Saturday's Game of the Week stood out because it gave the opportunity to see another team's ballpark and home uniform (back then seldom were Chicago games televised on the road). Fans did care, but it was more casual. Winning mattered, as seen in the direct relationships between attendance and standings. For instance, Philadelphia drew crowds of 30,000 in that summer of their infamous collapse. Later in the 60's, Cub numbers swelled to new heights also. But back in-the-day, the attitude was different, not indifferent, and not obsessive. Something lost, $omething gained.

On Waveland Avenue about one block west of Sheffield stands a Chicago fire station. As a first-grader, security is an issue. You couldn't feel much more secure knowing that firemen were as close as an Ernie Banks' home run.

It was near this fire station that the joy of June 30, 1964 was made complete. For it was in this general area that Cub players would amble from the clubhouse to their cars. Players actually exposed themselves to plenty of fans like me who could see, talk, and perhaps even get an autograph. Today an imposing white metal fence secludes players' cars from the fans. The barrier not only protects vehicles but sends a message to those on the other side of the fence: "We're not one of you."

As players strolled to their autos, some were gregarious and others were somber. Some liked the attention and others preferred anonymity. But even then I could almost always pick out the ballplayer. The way they carried themselves suggested that they were a tad more important than the average bear, because they were a Cub. It probably didn't damage their esteem and psyches to have hundreds of kids (and young moms) pleading for an autograph.

The real thrill of this day, even more than a Cubs' win and a near perfect game, was attaining Billy Williams' autograph. My favorite player, I kid you not. This was the one guy who my folks would give me updates on as I played in the alley behind our house. Billy Williams, whose baseball card was my Holy Grail. The guy who had the coolest stance and swing I tried to emulate (and poorly, him being a lefty and me being a righty), and this was way before anyone in the media called him "Sweet Swinging Billy." The guy who would spit out his gum and hit it with his bat just before entering the batter's box—what style! Yes, that guy.

My mom, in a moment of true inspiration, brought a ball and kept it in her purse (amazing things in that purse). Now it might have been due to other things in that purse, it might have been due to the horsehide, or it might have been something else entirely, but that ball was the sweetest smelling baseball I've ever come across. It possessed the most distinctive scent; even now, over forty years later, this faint fragrance on the ball provokes the sweetest memories. How fitting that the first autograph on this sweet-smelling ball should belong to sweet-swinging Billy.

Up close, Billy's demeanor was jovial and approachable. Here was a young man who looked about twelve and appeared to be having the time of his life. I liked him a lot before this day; after he signed my ball, I'd be loyal to him forever. I remember a few special Billy Williams' moments I saw in person: the time he drove a 10th inning homer to the catwalk in right to defeat the Big Red Machine; the time he smacked a ball off the upper deck scoreboard at the Old Comiskey Park in an exhibition game against the White Sox; the time he did a complete 360 to track down and catch Hank Aaron's long drive to preserve Kenny Holtzman's no-hitter; and the time he nailed a bittersweet homer against the Cardinals in September of '74 which proved to be his last as a Chicago Cub. All these episodes I witnessed first-hand. Yet none of them stand out as meeting Billy face-to-face and he being gracious enough to sign my ball.

When Billy played he seemed to be overlooked when compared to NL outfielders like Mays, Aaron, and Clemente. I was a great fan of his, but I knew he wasn't quite at their level. Consequently, I was pleasantly surprised that he did make it to Cooperstown years later. The official announcement that Billy was in the Hall-of-Fame was anti-climatic, however. To a young boy in the summer of '64, Billy Williams was already Hall-of-Fame material. And I had the autograph to prove it.

Other autographs would follow: great players, good players, and marginal players. But Billy Williams was the first and only autograph that I would receive that day. And I'm glad it worked out that way.

The only thing better than watching baseball is playing baseball. Pony League in suburban Hillside served 13-14 year olds. I was pitching one night against another Pony League team that featured Jay Martin, son of Cub (and former White Sox) player, J. C. Martin.

My family connected with the Martin clan in a number of ways. My sister had a major crush on J.C. I recall how she spoke admiringly about his eyes; a remark that thoroughly repulsed me. My dad, the typical White Sox fan, had this to say about J.C.: "His initials stand for 'Just Can't.'" I found this remark to be amusing and somewhat true. Investigating the back of his baseball card, his numbers are less than impressive. I think my dad was happier to see him in Cub pinstripes.

I got to know J.C. Martin a little bit through his son. J.C. happened to be watching our game that night as my team (the Dodgers) were trying to knock off Jay's team (the Sox). I don't recall the specifics, but I do know that I pitched and hit well. I think we won, but I wouldn't swear to it. (Allow me to digress: the daily pick-up games were much more fun than the Pony League games when adults were present. We loved the game we played during the day; we tolerated the game we played at night--I felt that parental presence took some of the fun away. During one of those morning pick-up games, Jay Martin hit a smash to me at shortstop. His bad-hop grounder found its way to my right cheekbone. A substantial and dramatic shiner appeared instantly. Jay was apologetic, but these things happen. Besides, it made for an interesting photo a couple days later as I donned the attire of an altar boy with this huge black eye.)

Anyway, a few days following my Pony League game with Jay Martin, I slither my way to the second row at Wrigley Field in search of autographs. Little did I know that I was about to receive the biggest compliment of my young life up to that point. As I was dodging the ushers and looking for players around the dugout, J. C. Martin made his way over to the stands.

Now I'm a big believer in the law of compensation. If you're not very good at one thing (physics) you're probably good at something else (computing batting averages). It's not a very scientific theory, but I've seen it played out time and again in real life. Well, J.C. Martin wasn't ever confused with Billy, Ted, or even Bernie Williams; but a nicer guy you'll never meet. (The acorn doesn't fall far from the tree—Jay Martin, who could have been a stuck-up kid of a major league dad, was a nice guy, too. I remember he showed me once the bat that Don Kessinger used to collect 6 hits in one game. Unfortunately, Kessinger broke it. Fortunately for us, Jay brought it to the neighborhood park and we spent about a half-hour staring at it and petting it).

Along comes J.C. smiling and cheerful as usual. As he stops to sign autographs, he looks up and notices me. A smile comes across his face as we make eye contact (boy, would my sister be jealous, but I think she ditched J.C. by then for Bobby Sherman). With dozens of fans surrounding him for a piece of his penmanship, he says to me in his southern drawl, "I remember you. You're a pretty good hitter and a pretty good pitcher." Now imagine what these words coming from a professional ball player would do for a kid not yet in high school. I floated back to my seat. I wonder if we realize how much positive influence one person can have over another.

JULY 4, 1964

"Watch your car, mister. Watch you car." These words were the second impression of my first White Sox game.

Pre-teens offered their services to my dad which seemed strange to me. Why would a car have to be watched? It wasn't going anywhere. It couldn't get into trouble. It didn't require babysitters as my two kid brothers did. So why watch it?

For a long time Comiskey Park held the stigma of an unsafe place. Over the years, I learned that this was more fiction than fact. Few, if any, seem to know how this perception got started, but a few suspects emerge.

Could it be the kids watching your car? (Let us watch your car for a few quarters, mister, or else ...). Perhaps the residents of the Comiskey Park neighborhood are responsible to minimize traffic and intrusions. Or maybe the management of the Chicago National League ball club promoted the myth that visits to 35th and Shields could be hazardous to your health. Possibly a combination of all of the above. Maybe none of the above. But whoever it was, they succeeded. Back in the sixties, if you were to talk to someone about Comiskey Park, within minutes the safety issue would be part of the conversation. It seldom, if ever, came up when talking about Wrigley Field. Yet I've heard that crime statistics for these two locales are not significantly different.

A big part of this myth had to do when games took place. The difference between Comiskey Park and Wrigley Field was not like night and day, it was night and day. When you factor in night games, huge quantities of beer consumption, and a more blue-collar clientele, there are bound to be a few more scuffles.

But safety at Comiskey Park and its neighborhood? Not a problem to me, ever.

"There they are, can you see them?"

"They" and "them" represent the first impression of my first White Sox game. The lights. When traveling by car as a kid throughout the Midwest, I kept look-out for two landmarks: the golden dome of Notre Dame and the lights of Comiskey Park. It wasn't quite like Gaspor and Melchior looking for a star, but the anticipation and excitement about seeing the tops of these two buildings was hardly containable.

Whereas Wrigley Field sneaks up on you, the lights at Comiskey Park give you advance notice. It tells you that something good is coming up. And with the way the Dan Ryan Expressway snakes southward, you were treated to different perspectives of these light structures. Later it became a contest: who can see the lights first? In some seasons this game would be more exciting than the one played inside the ballpark. For the 8 PM night games the lights would already be turned on, but not for the Fourth of July day game.

When you got close enough to see what was beneath these celebrated lights, the immensity of the building got your attention. White, clean, and traditional are adjectives to describe this place, once referred to as a baseball palace. Inside, cigar smoke and pillars abound. Ladies and little kids are not as commonplace as they are on the North Side. A sense of, "This is baseball, pal," permeates the grounds. No ivy on the wall, no pretty blue uniforms, no little cubby patch on the shoulder, no nonsense. (One frivolous exception surfaces in the person of Andy the Clown. This clown in the stands entertained fans with his long-winded cheers for players like Don Buford and Tommie McCraw. His bright red nose lit up, so he could be seen and heard from far away. Much fun.)

The coziness of Wrigley Field is in stark contrast to the vastness of Comiskey Park. Double-deck stands surround the entire playing surface and make the wind much less of a factor. Even a first-grader can tell that while homers can be the thing in Wrigley Field, outs are the attraction at Comiskey Park. Looking at this stadium, it reminded me of golf. If you stood at home plate and hit the ball as far as you could, waited until it stopped rolling and hit it again, and continued this process, by the fourth or fifth stroke you might reach the outfield seats.

The numerical dimensions don't tell the story. The 375 foot sign in the power alleys is only seven feet farther than the 368 sign in Wrigley Field, but it might as well be seven miles. At Comiskey Park, wind-blown homers didn't happen. Unless your surname was Foxx, Mantle, or Bunyan, forget about it. Comiskey Park was big.

A story has been told how White Sox officials of this era kept baseballs in the freezer so they wouldn't travel very far come game time. By looking at offensive production from this era, it seems quite believable. Legend has it that Harmon Killebrew, powerful possessor of the prodigious long-ball, once got all of a frozen puck, er, fastball. The humble Killer began his home run trot, only to see his mammoth drive end up in the left fielder's glove a few feet shy of the warning track.

The center field scoreboard at Comiskey Park featured two attractions that caught my eye. The first was the lineup of that day's game. How intriguing it was to try to figure out the batting orders for both teams without referring to your program (scorecards at Wrigley, programs at Comiskey). Walking to our seats, I studied this code and tried my best to decipher it.

Player #	Position
8	3B	This meant Pete Ward would be playing third base and batting clean-up. He was a legitimate threat.
3	RF	Unfortunately, this was NOT posted. Floyd Robinson, probably the best hitter on the team, would not be starting. Must be a lefty pitching for the other team.
15	C	Too bad my brother Mark isn't here. His favorite player, J. McNertney would be catching this day. His playing would not only make my brother happy, but given his anemic numbers, the opposing team might be glad, too.

In the pre-designated hitter days, the key to the entire lineup was the ninth slot. If you followed the Sox closely, the ninth slot was not automatically the pitcher's spot. I remember keeping score of a game when the Sox visited New York, and the pitcher, Gary Peters, hit seventh. I wonder how this set with the players who hit eighth and ninth that day.

But this day the pitcher did bat ninth. When I saw "43 P" at the bottom of the line-up, the other eight previous positions were almost irrelevant. With Gary Peters, #43, pitching, I liked the Sox chances. If the team could somehow manage to scratch out a run, we most likely would go home happy. Peters in 1964 dominated, especially at home with those frozen balls.

On July 4, 1964 the White Sox offense managed to score four runs off a young Cleveland southpaw, Sam McDowell. This proved to be three runs more than necessary. McDowell threw the ball very hard, hence the nickname, "Sudden Sam." Strikeouts in abundance—21 altogether, with 13 whiffs by Sox batsmen (12 credited to McDowell). Even more impressive was the scarcity of hits—only 4 by the Sox and 3 by the Tribe. This made for a grand total of 10 hits (nine of which were singles) by 4 teams in my first two games.

So how did the White Sox get four runs on three singles and a double? The answer is in control, or lack thereof. McDowell walked 11 batters. It was reminiscent of a fast-pitching game, complete with a rubber ball and a square that was supposed to be the strike zone scrawled on a wall. (If someone owning the property came out to complain, the response of the players was to run or hop on the bikes and pedal fast). It was baseball's version of one-on-one, pitcher vs. hitter with very few, if any, fielders. The game consisted of walks and strike-outs. Once every two innings or so would the rubber ball would be hit. And when that happened the ball frequently spun two feet in front of the batter looking like an egg. It was the game of choice when players were lacking. The downside was that it took about seven batters before someone would throw his arm out, bringing the match to an abrupt end.

With McDowell pitching, it almost seemed that fielders and bats were superfluous. One would either look at four balls or suffer through three strikes. Remarkable, especially considering how unimposing the White Sox lineup was. But throwing strikes is one of those things that's often easier said than done. Just ask Steve Blass. Only two of the starting eight hit safely—Pete Ward and Joe Cunningham (his was the double). Al Weis off the bench and Gary Peters himself collected the other two knocks (maybe it's not such a crazy idea to hit him seventh; I do remember him being used as a pinch-hitter on several occasions). McDowell's defeat conjures up two pearls of great wisdom:

"We have met the enemy and it is ourselves."

"Those #*!#* bases-on-balls!"

Another memory of this game was the weather. It was very chilly by Fourth of July standards. Seems strange because a few days earlier, the Cubs played in very warm temperatures on the north side (further from the equator). It was so brisk that day that my sister, who seldom told me much of anything except to be quiet, observed how goose bumps were prevalent over our exposed arms and legs. (My sister Jean did have two questions for me at our first Cub game. She leaned over and asked when the game was going to start as the Cubs came to bat in the fourth inning. Later, she wanted to know if the Cubs were the team in blue. And they were playing the REDS. A baseball expert she was not). With regards to climate, I noticed how much warmer it was outside the ballpark after the game, especially in your car, than it was sitting in the shade of the grandstands.

Our seats that day provided us with an excellent view of these extraordinary pitching performances. The way we ended up there provided me with an early lesson in Chicago politics. My dad once worked as an Andy Frain usher for Chicago sporting events. A former co-worker recognized my father, and switched our seat location from general admission to the reserved grandstand section right behind home plate. Obviously the ushers in blue took care of each other. It definitely was an upgrade. You see, the general admission ticket got you into the pale green section down the foul lines or in the outfield. A reserved grandstand seat meant a place in the red section located behind the poles from base to base. The bright green seats made me green with envy—those were the box seats to witness the game up close and personal. The bleachers in Comiskey were not famous like the bleachers in Wrigley; on the South Side a ticket there got you in the ballpark, but just barely. You ended up in deep center field; I think 5 ballplayers ever reached those seats, some 450 feet from home plate. With binoculars the number of the center fielder could be deciphered. On this holiday, my dad, sister, and I, along with 12,158 other customers perched our posteriors on these multi-colored seats.

The scoreboard in center-field has been described, but the vastness of the ballpark allowed for a second and more efficient scoreboard on the right field façade. Here you got runs, hits, errors, for the White Sox and "Visitor". It also told interested parties balls, strikes, outs, and who was batting—that's about it and that's all I really needed to know. The monstrosity in center field had lots of advertising (I remember "Bowman" and "Coca-Cola" logos), an inning by inning account of the game at hand, scores from both leagues (the Cubs always seemed to be losing), and a message board called "Sox-o-gram." This informed us of what group was at the game (sometimes the entire crowd could be considered a group unto itself), the records of the starting pitchers, upcoming promotions, and other stuff that didn't interest a first-grader. My preference was the unassuming scoreboard in right rather than the vast message center in center. Besides, during sunny day games you couldn't even make out the words or numerals in center field, anyway. Night games were a different story. Yet all eyes would be fixed toward this direction in the event that a White Sox player smacked a home run. Should this happen, fans were treated to an exploding scoreboard. Lights blinked on and off in circular and angular directions, fireworks ascending a few stories high, and sonic booms from nowhere really rocked the place. To see this happen was truly worth the price of admission. As a boy, I was much obliged to Bill Veeck who was the mastermind of this entertainment. As I got older, I applauded White Sox management for their ability to pull off this mini-show in spite of great inactivity and potential rust. For instance, Pete Ward led the team in homers in 1968 with a grand total of 15. The purchasing agent probably never worried about inventory levels. In fact, I'm surprised the White Sox didn't use it as a promotion: first 10,000 fans will receive a set of fireworks, courtesy of White Sox banjo hitters.

Turning back to the action on the field, I recall that this was one of the few days when the visitor's uniform looked better than the home team. The Sox had simple uniforms: bleached white with black pinstripes and dark socks (I couldn't figure that out—dark socks for the White Sox?). On the back, their numbers were rather small so that the names could be placed just above them. The S-O-X on the hat and helmet was angled and stylish. Overall, not hard on the eyes at all. But this day these outfits to a back seat to the Tribe. Vivid red jumped off the Indians' sleeves (remember it was not a warm day). And I know this is very politically incorrect, but I'll say it anyway, knowing that I'm likely to get fined, censored, and/or imprisoned: that famous Indian face that was worn on the jersey was one of the coolest things on the planet. Seeing that logo reminded me of baseball, Peter Pan, and happiness. I also think of baseball cards and Bazooka bubble gum because it seemed I got more Indian players in my packs of cards than any other team.

On this day the uniform was about the only thing the Cleveland team had going for them. Aside from the McDowell K's, the only thing worthy of note was a long fly ball (frozen?) clobbered by Leon Wagner, who had the coolest nickname on the team with the coolest logo. "Daddy Wags" hit a drive to the warning track in deep right; in Wrigley Field it probably would have broken a window on Sheffield Ave. But for the Tribe's attack, that was it, and their futility was due to the performance of the 1963 Rookie of the Year, Gary Peters. If poets could pitch they'd look like Peters. I often wondered, with a fair amount of envy, why lefties always looked so much smoother than righties. First it was Gary Peters, then a little later it was Tommy John (who, by the way, was on the visiting team this day. Imagine a pitching staff of McDowell, John, Luis Tiant, and Sonny Siebert). When you saw such sound and effortless mechanics in Peters' delivery, how could a hitter be successful? Hawk Harrelson once told me that when he hit against Peters, he ended driving the ball into his left ankle time and again, because his ball would break so sharply in that direction.

A telling stat from this era was the White Sox earned run averages. In 1964, Peters would go on to win 20 games, and lead the league with a 1.98 E.R.A. Another hurler from this time, Joe Horlen, posted a 2.43 E.R.A., yet had a losing record! I guess that happens when leading home run hitters crank out 15, and the LEADING batting averages from one year was .241 (a tie between Don Buford and Ken Berry).

As mentioned earlier, the 1-0 lead which the Sox held from the 4th to the 8th inning seemed pretty insurmountable. I recall how the Sox defense complemented its pitching— when you looked at just the final score, you didn't know if it was a baseball game or a Blackhawk game. (The Cubs, on the other hand, had some final scores more fitting for a Bear game). A run for the White Sox was about as big as a goal was from Bobby Hull. The Sox added three more runs in the 8th, a hat trick, to put this one in the win column.

As in my first Cub game, the real excitement of the day was not so much the game but an autograph. I was fortunate to get a Sox player to sign his name on the sweet-smelling ball that Mr. Williams already signed. His name was Frank Kreutzer. Frank was a young lefty who wore glasses and didn't see a lot of action. In fact, he would soon be exiled to the Washington Senators. But he was kind enough to sign my ball that day. I never heard of him, so once I got my ball back, I turned to my dad and asked him if Kreutzer was any good. My dad said yes (a lie, but what would you tell your kid?) and I was thrilled once again.

Let's compare these two ballplayers: Billy Williams and Frank Kreutzer. Williams made All-Star teams and eventually the Hall-of-Fame. Kreutzer was lucky to be on a major league roster and would have to buy a ticket like you and me to get into Cooperstown. Yet, both were heroes to me. Consider this: how many people have you met for just a moment over 40 years ago and never met again do you still remember? I have two.

GAME 3 July 22, 1964

Most of the games I saw in person in the 1960's were as memorable as the first two, with one being downright famous. Being from Chicago, I've grown accustomed to leaving the ballpark disappointed, frustrated, and/or angered. Surprisingly, however, the '64-'69 years of going to games produced more than my share of happy trips home.

In fact, after my first two games I was beginning to think that Chicago teams may lose on TV, but not when I'm there in person. Call it first-grade cockiness, inexperience, or idealism, but that's what shutouts could do to you. "If they don't score, we can't lose," a mantra many coaches have lived by over the years. Not only did my heroes in both leagues win their games, but they allowed these two Buckeye teams only a handful of singles with zero runs scored. I ask you what are the chances of a Cubs and White Sox pitcher tossing a complete game shutout within a few days of each other in this era? My opinion of the Sox and Cubs was getting pretty inflated, thinking that our opposition was nothing more than the Washington Generals to our Chicago Globe-trotters. I'd soon learn the hard way that not all games would be so glorious. Early success like this reminds me of the student who foolishly earns straight A's in first grade—parent and teacher expectations hit the stratosphere for the poor kid.

So early success spoiled me. Not only was a defeat unacceptable, I didn't think that the opponent would even score. And although the Cubs were terrible in the mid-60's and the Sox quite competitive (up to '67, 17 consecutive winning seasons), Comiskey Park would be the scene of my first heartbreak.

The Los Angeles Angels came to town. Not the California, Anaheim, or Los Angeles Angels of Anaheim, but the Los Angeles Angels. This was my first experience with baseball under the lights. Since nite games back then didn't start until 8 PM, we had time to go out for dinner in Chinatown beforehand. Almost too much for me to bear—my first nite game and my first set of chopsticks. I succeeded in getting very little Egg Foo Young from the plate to my mouth. Knowing that a ball game was imminent, I was too excited to eat. Besides, I had to save room for fortune cookies and popcorn. Other meal recollections were the folks and decorations in the restaurant—both very pleasant and friendly.

The first impression of this game: the Angels' cap. It had a halo on top of it. Not really a halo, more like a white circle, but it was definitely cool enough for me. I also got to thinking about this team's name. Wouldn't God be for the Angels? And if so, how were the Sox ever going to win? And if God rooted for the Angels, shouldn't I do the same? Some serious theological dilemmas which lasted up to the first inning; then the Angels became my mortal enemy.

To some folks, the Angels are an expansion team. A funny thing about expansion teams—they're only expansion if people remember when they didn't exist. That's why I never viewed teams like the Angels, Twins, Mets, and Astros (Colt 45's) as expansion clubs. The Padres, Expos, Royals, Marlins, Brewers, etc. are expansion teams and will always be deemed as such. But not the Angels—like God, they always were.

Soon the lights would take effect, but now they were on and it wasn't even dark. As the game moved along the lights seemed to yield a brighter playing surface than the sunshine. I remember looking at Joe Horlen hurl and wonder if he looked the same during the day. On offense, the Sox helmets fascinated me with their glimmer and glow. And now that monstrous scoreboard in center field could actually be read with no strain on the eyes. The Sox-o-gram messages continuously poured out mundane information (maybe day games weren't so bad). Also, the fans could more easily decipher how the Cubs were faring on the road (another liability since they were losing to the Giants). The red dots indicated which team was currently batting; the numbers, of course, referred to inning, score, and pitcher. Hardly any of this intriguing information was available to me on that sunny and chilly 4th of July.

Horlen, wearing #20 on his bright white uniform, delivered the ball with a smooth and unassuming motion, a la Bill Hands of the Cubs. Joe also had a peculiar habit of chewing during the game—not gum nor tobacco, but tissue paper. I wonder if kids in Chicago or Texas (Joe's home state) ever picked up on this. Horlen had a reputation of being a tough-luck pitcher; one who pitches well but doesn't get the win. Would that happen tonight?

Much to my delight, the Sox exploded for two runs in the very first inning. If this were 1968, and Horlen was pitching, it's likely that the final score would be 2 to 1.88, given the Sox paltry offense and Joe's low ERA that year. Unfortunately, this was not 1968 and Joe did not go the distance.

Early in the game, Don Buford hit a ball that passed third base in fair ground but then rolled into foul territory. Oh well, I sighed, perhaps he can get a ball to stay fair. But then I noticed Buford (or Pooh-ford, as my dad not-so-affectionately called him) stayed on second base. My dad tried to explain to me the fairness of the foul line, but I was still confused. How can you still be running the bases if the ball you hit is in foul ground? I learned an important lesson that day—a double, like life, doesn't always seem fair.

These two runs seemed like plenty for our heroes. Horlen's pitching line: 1 run, 3 hits, 1 walk, 8 strikeouts, 7 innings. Today, unfortunately, the game has evolved to "turn things over to the bullpen" to shorten the game. With this philosophy has emerged another sad stat: the blown save. In the 60's baseball did not avoid complete games like the plague, and it's probable that Mr. Horlen would have stayed on had it not been for his aching shoulder. So Al Lopez, esteemed manager of the White Sox, summoned in the "good doctor", Hoyt Wilhelm.

Hoyt Wilhelm. Who would name their kid Hoyt? But there are things far more important about him than his name. For one thing he was older than my parents, for Pete Ward's sake! Here's a guy older than guys playing in *Old Timer's games*. I used to think that Sox relievers were brought in to pitch on a golf cart because of Hoyt. Better a golf cart than a walker.

Then there's Hoyt's offensive productivity. Hoyt hit a homer (this sounds like something from Dr. Seuss) in his very first game. Not common for anyone, let alone a pitcher. But here's what is almost too good to be true— in his 21 year career, Hoyt **never** homered again. You can look it up. It's stuff like that which makes me proud to be a baseball fan. One can only speculate, but perhaps Hoyt suffered from over-confidence. Like the kid who gets straight A's early, that "too much too soon" syndrome can be a killer. Compare the ratios for these Hall-of-Famers:

Babe Ruth	1 HR every 11.8 at bats
Hank Aaron	1 HR every 16.4 at bats
Hoyt Wilhelm	1 HR every 432 at bats

One could look to the Law of Averages and argue that Hoyt is due for another long ball around his 425th at bat, but as Chicago fans know, you can't put too much stock in the law of averages.

When Hoyt pitched on any given night, the majority of sober fans (about a dozen or so) could throw the ball faster. His and Phil Niekro's were the most famous knuckleballs. When he came into the game, the White Sox catcher and my sister's heart throb, J.C. Martin, would get a special mitt to try to catch his "butterfly" pitch. This glove looked the size of a Volkswagen.

The best thing about Hoyt was a family matter. I knew his kid. I don't mean to be a name-dropper and

I didn't know many sons of professional athletes, just two. But they happened to be the boys of the White Sox battery—Jay Martin and Jimmy Wilhelm. Jimmy was a pitcher, naturally, and the Little League team for which he played wore red shirts. I think they were the Dodgers. Aside from being a good pitcher, and starting pitcher no less, he had this tendency to tilt his head when looking at the catcher's target, just like his old man. I later found out that Hoyt's head tilting helped him see the catcher's signs better. Jimmy at the age of 9 could throw faster than his dad, but the only way he'd get into the Hall-of-Fame would be by purchasing a ticket. Once inside he could look up his father.

Hall-of-Famer or not, Jimmy's dad tore my heart to pieces that night. The Sox held the lead for the entire game. Then with two outs to victory, Jim Fregosi (an eventual Sox manager) singled and Willie Smith (an eventual Cub opening day hero in '69) reached with a hit-by-pitch. This brought up Buck Rodgers who was neither a future Cub nor Sox player, but still had a cool name. He drove in the tying run. But what hoyt even more than that was how the Angels scored the winning run—a passed ball. That colossal catcher's glove couldn't handle one of Wilhelm's knucklers. As an Angel raced in from third, I had a devil of a time holding back the tears.

When the Sox failed to score in the 9th, I couldn't take it anymore. I let loose with what seemed to be an hour and twenty minute tear delay. Those damn Angels. But my folks came up with something that I never forgot; they took me out for ice cream on an airplane. That's right, a huge, grounded airplane that was really a restaurant somewhere on the West/Southwest side of Chicago. First time I was ever on an airplane outside of Kiddieland. I devoured vanilla ice cream with whip cream (passed on the cherry) and the tears eventually subsided. Considering it all—Chinatown, first nite game, and ice cream on an airplane—it wasn't so bad. I just wished knuckle balls weren't so hard to catch.

GAME 4 August 29, 1964

"Hey, kid, do you have the Mets on your jacket?" (Much laughter ensued).

Do you remember those red baseball jackets that every boy seemed to have growing up in the 60's? The one with the team logo inside a baseball patch? I wore mine a lot; a clever way for my mom to get me to wear more clothing on cool days. Well as I was deciding which pack of baseball cards to buy at the local grocery store, this young employee comes up to me and asks the above question. Quickly I pointed to my right-hand pocket area to the logo with buildings and sky-scrapers in the background, the Mets. I wondered why several people around him were laughing because it seemed like a pretty normal request to me; in fact, it's a question I'd ask myself. Little did I know (but obviously they did) that this team called the Mets recently lost 120 games in a season.

The Mets were atrocious, much worse than the Cubs. That's bad. My mom probably remembered my distraught reaction to the White Sox defeat, so it would be prudent to watch the Cubs play a team they should beat. With the Mets in town and second grade about to begin, why not try our luck.

Mom and I strolled to Central Avenue (56 blocks west of State Street) and caught a bus, courtesy of the Chicago Transit Authority. Then we traveled north by northeast on a journey that required several transfers. The bus ride was delightful. The CTA had electric buses back then with these two huge rods sticking up in the air and being connected to wires that ran parallel overhead. Every so often you'd see some sparks fly as the bus veered to the curb to pick up some passengers. It's been said that these poles occasionally would disconnect from their overhead juice supply, resulting in a traffic mess of major proportions. No such mishap today, shucks. But it was on this trip that I'd be introduced to a favorite landmark.

Heading eastbound on Addison Street inside a CTA bus will never be confused with Germany's Autobahn. Plenty of traffic, frequent bus stops, no left turn lanes and stoplights every 45 feet or so makes for deliberate travel. But people didn't seem as hyper or rushed back then for some reason, even in a big place like Chicago. On the upside, you had a great opportunity for serious sight-seeing. And what a sight I saw, FRANKSVILLE. I've no idea what the food was like, but on Addison west of Wrigley Field stood this hot dog place. The mobile outdoor sign had this railroad engineer perched on this hot dog like it was a train. As he sat on his bun as a picture of tranquility, I marveled from below. Fine piece of marketing. This choo-choo Charlie was right up there with those enormous plastic soft serve ice cream cone replicas that stood atop ice cream stands. Remember those?

When we arrived at Wrigley Field, would a game against the Mets be anti-climactic to a ride on the CTA? No way. For one thing, there would be no color clash today. The gray and blue of the visiting Mets, with a hint of mild orange versus the royal blue pinstripes of the Cubs. I hope that I wouldn't get confused by that and start rooting for the wrong team.

Next were the names of the Met ballplayers. First, they had a guy in the middle infield with the name of Klaus (I think his first name was Bobby; he had an older brother named Billy who played primarily in the American League). Think of the fun with puns you can have with that, "Hey mom, I went to the Cub game in August and guess who I saw? Santo/Klaus." They had an outfielder with two first names: Joe Christopher. (The antithesis of that would be a player with no first names, like Morgan Ensberg). Batting clean-up in center field was a player who would eventually be a fan favorite with the Cubs, Jim Hickman. For the longest time I got him confused with Dobie Gillis, who was played by Dwayne Hickman. George Altman, now with the Mets, represented the past and future for the Cubs. He did play for them earlier and would later play with them again. Big George was also one of the first Americans to play ball in Japan. And then you had the original Met. Can you name him? A clue for those who can't: he has the same birthday as mine, November 8. Need another? OK, he was seen on Sesame Street playing pepper with a couple of teammates as kids were learning how to count. Here's your final clue: he was around for the run of the Amazin' Mets in 1969. That's right, Ed Kranepool. And what could be said that hasn't already been said, over and over, about the manager, Casey Stengel. A rancid team, these Mets, but loaded with plenty of trivial tidbits to pass the time.

Now the Cubs had plenty of characters of their own. Picture a relief pitcher that was heavy into hypnotism. That sort of thing was pretty rare in the blue-collar days of tobacco chewing and get-a-job-in-the-winter behaviors. This hypnotic hurler was Bill Faul. And he wasn't very good. Neither was a battery mate at the time, Vic Roznovsky. Try getting a second grader to spell that name correctly on a scorecard. Fortunately, that problem didn't present itself too often because Vic usually sat in the bullpen waiting to warm up the next reliever.

All in all, this had all the makings of an evenly matched game between two lousy teams. It's a shame someone had to win. (But let it be the Cubs because crying on the CTA bus heading home would be less than honorable).

It took ten innings but less than 2 ½ hours due to fewer pitching changes and commercials. All those minutes and bus transfers were worth it, because the Cubs won, 4-3. I wonder how many games the Cubs won that year when Williams and Santo both went hitless. Not many, I suppose, but now I got to witness two. The lefty starter for the Cubs, Dick Ellsworth, worked all ten innings. I can't see that happening today. Ellsworth gave up a two-run bomb to Hickman in the first, and the opposing pitcher, Galen Cisco, singled in a run in the 6th. I noticed how the pitcher slipped into a bright, blue Met jacket and ran the bases in such attire—pretty cool. The Cub offense was led by Jimmy Stewart (again) and Mr. Cub, Ernie Banks. Ernie homered that day, the 371st of his career, surpassing Gil Hodges. For the season, it was # 18 for Ernie, in kind of a down year. (I'd later learn that Ernie struggled with his health issues in '64). But the big hit that day was by Ellis Burton in the 10th inning, which drove in Stewart with the game winner. Ellis Narrington Burton may have only batted .190 that year and drove in seven runs, but he was okay with me.

Just for fun, I'd like to know how many times in sports that the winning team did not lead until the very last play of the game. That's precisely what happened in this game after the Mets grabbed a 2-0 lead in the first inning. The Cubs never led until Burton's hit in the final at-bat of the game. Tough to take if you're the losing team, to be ahead or tied for 99% of the game, only to lose in the end. If the Cubs had lost such a game, I bet a certain 2nd grader would need some serious consolation, again. But all's well that end's well, as Shakespeare and Jack Brickhouse would say. The heartache from the Gotham Mets would have to wait a few more years.

A closing thought on the complete game. It's probably always been the case where the current older generation thinks that the current younger generation is a tad soft. But I can't help but notice that in my first four games, I witnessed five complete games. There are some teams that won't have five complete games *all season*. Is it the delicacy of arms, pitching specialists, pitch counts, righty/lefty match-ups, more revenue for more pitching change commercials, all of the above or none of the above? Whatever the reason, something lost and something gained.

1964 Postseason

Civil unrest in the 60's. As a little kid, I was pretty oblivious to all that. But the '64 World Series provided a fairly clear dichotomy on racial composition. The powerful and white Yankees (save for Al Downing and Elston Howard) opposed by the quick and integrated Cardinals.

Looking at the rosters you'd find no shortage of baseball icons: Gibson & Ford, Flood & Mantle, Brock & Maris (could have been Broglio & Maris, in which case St. Louis might have been watching the Series on TV). And don't forget the intriguing match-up that sounds like a divorce case: Boyer vs. Boyer. How would you like to be a parent of Ken or Clete? Imagine if you could combine Ken's MVP offense with Clete's sparkling defense. You'd probably end up with Mike Schmidt.

This was the first World Series that I remember. And what I remember most about this Series occurred at a friend's house about one block away on Laramie Avenue. It was the Sunday afternoon game; back then all games were played in the afternoon. Who remembers the year of the first night game? (Hint: it took place in Pittsburgh, 11 years after the Bucs beat the Yankees in 1960). Since all games were during afternoons, smuggling small transistor radios into school was something done by kids who didn't even like baseball—just an excuse for trying to get away with something. No transistor needed this day, but I wasn't glued to the television either. I was playing with my pal, Larry Martin, when his dad, who spoke with this neat Irish brogue, informed me that Ken Boyer just delivered a grand slam. We all were quite happy. It's not so much we liked the Cardinals; we loathed the Yankees (the only team that finished ahead of the Chisox that year).

Boyer's slam was huge (final score that day was 4-3), Tim McCarver's play was clutch, but the difference in this Series (as in '67 and almost '68) was Bob Gibson. Even at my young age I could tell Gibson was special. He scared me, and I was just watching on TV. Imagine trying to hit against this guy. With guts and a glare, he hung in there on fumes to outlast the Yankees in Game 7. Who would have guessed that it would be a dozen years until we'd see those Yankee pinstripes in the Series again? I wonder what kind of odds you'd get if you bet that the New York Mets would win the World Series before the New York Yankees would.

My favorite Bob Gibson moment was not in the World Series, though. It happened during a regular season game when he was pitching against the Pirates. Consider this match-up: Gibson pitching and Roberto Clemente batting. Could baseball, sports, life be any more competitive and proud? Again, I didn't see it first hand, but I remember that Clemente broke Gibson's leg with a line drive. For most athletes you'd expect to see trainer, ambulance, and last rites on the pitcher's mound. Gibson did eventually leave the game, but not before finishing the inning!

Change was in the air at the end of this season. Aside from the Yankee fall from glory, parity became the order of the day. Five different champions would be crowned between 1965-1969. Neither local team would be playing fall ball, but notable changes were taking place on both sides of town. The Sox came very close in '64, finishing one game behind New York. If it hadn't been for that stupid Angels game back in ...oh, what's the use!

GAME 5: July 3, 1965

Two trips to the ballpark this year, both on the North side, and both good ones. Chicago Cubs vs. San Francisco Giants on a warm summer night. (Can you find the error in the previous sentence?)

The first impression on my going-into-third-grade mind dealt with the Giant uniform. How could they possibly fit that many letters across their jersey? And not only fit, but come through as tidy and attractive. The touch of orange and black, with the 'S' and 'F' intersecting smartly on their cap, resulted in a sharp road uniform.

But there's no doubt as to what the real attraction was for the Giants—Willie Mays. You feared him, and since he didn't play for my team, I didn't like him. But great players transcend boos and cheers. You watch the all-time greats to appreciate how well the game can be played. Unfortunately, due to a minor injury that day, I never got the chance to see the "Say-Hey" kid. Aaron—yes, Clemente—yes, Kaline—yes, Mantle—yes, Killebrew—yes, Frank & Brooks Robinson—yes & yes, Mays—no. That was the bad news. The good news is that the Cubs stood a much better chance of winning the ballgame.

Larry Jackson dominated the league in '64. He finished 13 games over .500 (24-11) on a team that finished 10 games below .500 (76-86). He started 38 games, led the league in wins, worked **298** innings, 19 complete games, finished with a 3.14 ERA, and of course, tossed a near-perfect game. But 1965 was a different story for the guy from Idaho. Not to make excuses, but did you ever notice how rare it is for a starting pitcher to have success over an <u>extended</u> period of time with the Cubs? Outside of Fergie Jenkins, Greg Maddux, & Rick Reuschel who do you have? "I'd, rather sell ice cubes to an Eskimo than pitch in Wrigley Field," Don Sutton once quipped at a baseball clinic. So it went for Jackson in '65—from a 24-game winner to a 21-game loser.

Jackson's struggles notwithstanding, the Cubs won that day (not night) by a 4-1 margin. You could say that the second tier Hall-of-Famers homered in the game, Willie McCovey and Billy Williams (in lieu of Mays & Banks). Another homer to right by the Cub catcher, Ed Bailey, sealed the deal for Chicago.

Did you ever wonder why insignificant remarks and episodes may be engraved in the memory bank forever, while there are times people can't remember the ages of their children? For instance, I remember an older fan assuring me that it's a good thing that the Cubs keep getting the "leading lady" by recording force plays at second base. I really had no clue what he meant at the time; I was just happy that the Cub defense kept Giant runners out of scoring position.

Names of Giant personnel grabbed my attention. They had a skilled third basemen, Jim Ray Hart. How rhythmic to have an extra name thrown in, and a short one at that. The Frisco manager, who would later become a Cub manager, made me hungry: Herman Franks. I couldn't help but think of barbecue grills and mustard whenever

I heard his name. 2/3 of the Alou brothers were in the lineup that day, Matty and Jesus. And most compelling of all, I saw a Japanese ballplayer pitch for the Giants in relief. His name was Masonori Murakami. For some reason, he scared me more than Willie Mays. Perhaps I saw too many war movies as a kid.

While Murakami was pitching, the Cubs did something almost unthinkable—they unleashed a running game. In the 8th inning the Cubs swiped two bases, on the same play! It's not every day you see the Cubs steal one base, let alone two (how did that Brock guy ever turn out?) Murakami's delivery to home must have taken forever. Whatever, the larceny paid dividends, as Ernie singled home both runners.

4-1. Now I ask you not to laugh, but for many years that has been one of my favorite baseball scores, provided my team has the "4". Here's why: a 4-1 game meant that you enjoyed some success on offense, but didn't make a mockery of the other team's pitching staff. The 4-1 score also suggests that pitching and defense were alive and well for the good guys. 4-1, not too close, but not a blow-out either. Yes sir, I've always liked a 4-1 score, and I'm sure it has something to do with the outcome of this Cub-Giant game in July of '65. My last memory of this day was looking up at my favorite scoreboard in center field and seeing a "4" under inning #10 for the Cubs, and the "1" registered in that same frame for San Francisco, as all the other numbers were being removed. Life is good.

GAME 6 September 2, 1965

How long would it take to hit 400 home runs? When you do some number crunching, it's an impressive milestone. You'd have to average about one homer per week for about 15 seasons. Or you could double up and hit two per week for nearly 8 seasons. Either way, sounds like you'd have to have two things going for you: skill and durability. Not many ballplayers reach this mark or come anywhere close. But on September 2, 1965 Ernie Banks accomplished this feat. Not only were O'Donnell's present to testify, but we have it on tape. That's right, my mom brought this cumbersome piece of camera equipment to the game. I guess she thought history might be made that day. And you can see it, not the clearest picture, but sure enough, there's Mr. Cub rounding second base after he banged out another. Look carefully and you can make out a couple of teammates trotting ahead of him.

The day was sunny and bright and our seats were in the left field bleachers. These were the pre-bleacher bum days when obscenities, drunkenness and lewd behavior was not as common. As a kid the bleachers were not my favorite place to sit. I know this categorizes me as a "square", but I liked the bleachers less as I got older. Many of my friends loved it, but it was just too far from the action for my taste. An occasional long fly in your direction just doesn't cut it. But I guess the funds were low at this time, so it was out to the cheap seats ($1.00 for an adult ticket). What the heck, I'd sit on the scoreboard to see a game.

What fashions do you remember from the 60's? The white go-go boots, medallions, Nehru and tie-dyed shirts? My sister wore something that day that was ahead of its time, a pair of sunglasses that had a very narrow, horizontal lens running from one eye to the other. White plastic encircled the lens, both above and below, and the look was something punk-rockers would adapt some 15 years later. It would be perfect for a group like "Devo." Now when it comes to fashion, I probably come close to

Barney Rubble or Barney Fife, but even I thought they were pretty cool. A vendor in the bleachers liked them too; I remember him asking my sister if she could really see out of those things. You could, and you didn't have to squint at all with the sun beating down on you.

Sitting in the left center field bleachers placed us in close proximity to the Cardinals' Curt Flood and the Cubs' Don Landrum. The vivid red of the St. Louis uniform has to be the best in baseball. It was brighter than the red on the Reds, that's how good it was. And for some reason, I thought the black ballplayers looked especially sharp—guys like Flood, Bill White, Gibson, and Brock (who would look even better in Cub blue, but oh well ...).

Speaking of Flood, he had a miserable game, and the bleacher crowd would not let him forget this. At one point a navy blue superball made its way out to him. This was also the time prior to baskets stretched out along the top of the outfield wall to discourage such shenanigans from taking place. (I wonder how many fly outs have turned into home runs because of that basket? One friend who is a Sox fan and Cub hater suggests that it's always the Cub hitters who seem to have those fly balls drop in that blasted basket). Superballs were a novelty back then and very popular. Throwing such an item at Flood was definitely foolish, inexcusable, and has no place in our national pass time—you could end up losing it. As a third grader I could understand why fans pleaded so earnestly with Mr. Flood to return it, and I don't remember if he did or not. If I were him I would have used some serious wit and told the kid, "Finders keepers, losers weepers."

These super balls and groovy sunglasses provided a fitting backdrop for the pitching style of the Cardinals' southpaw. His name was Curt Simmons, he was older than dirt, and the Cubs would acquire him as he got older still. But his trademark was a quivering, spastic-like motion with his right foot as he delivered the baseball. If you've seen him pitch you know what I'm talking about. If you haven't, sorry, there's no one around that I can really compare him to. As a kid, anything that unorthodox left a lasting impression. His style was not as famous as the Marichal kick or the Tiant twist, but it was still pretty weird.

Weird or no, Simmons' mechanics didn't bother the Cubs much that day. They got to him for five runs in five innings, which included the milestone by Banks. His homer came with two men on base, which permits us to reflect upon some baseball philosophy. Is the best offense a three- run homer, as Earl Weaver contends? Throughout the years the Cubs have lived and died (mostly died) with the home run. But I'm not so sure it's been the three-run home run. On base percentage plus power equals productive offense. Regardless of whatever offensive strategy to which you subscribe, this much is true: the big inning is crucial. Allow me to digress: Did you know that the winning team usually scores more runs in one inning than the losing team scores in the entire game? Take this game as evidence: the Cubs tally four times in the fourth on their way to a 5-3 victory (another favorite score of mine). The thing is the big inning—stay away from them on defense, grab them on offense, and I'll take my chances from there.

Bob Hendley pitched well for the home team. Any true Cub fan knows what Hendley's claim to fame (or infamy) is. He pitched a one-hit masterpiece later that month in '65 against the Los Angeles Dodgers. That's the good news. The bad news is that this one hit was one more than the Cubs got on offense. In fact, Hendley's gem was up against a perfect game tossed by Sandy Koufax. Talk about bad timing. An "A" for the day if you can name the only player to get a hit that night? (Some clues: he also played for the Cubs, he was an outfielder, and his nickname was "Sweet Lou". Give up? Lou Johnson).

Turning our attention back to the Sep. 2nd game, we discover that Hendley's victory was not a complete game. Ted Abernathy pitched the 8th **and** 9th innings to earn the save. (When was the last time you saw a two inning save?) Abernathy got my attention for two reasons. First was the way he threw the ball. Underhand. Not softball underhand, but submarine underhand. This style was mimicked by me endlessly in the back alley with a rubber ball against a wall. Ted was good, he pitched for several teams and usually got people out at the end of the game. The other remarkable thing about "Ab" was his handwriting. Ted was kind enough to sign my ball after the game, but it was a good thing he didn't go to my school. The nuns would have had him work extra innings after school to improve his sloppy penmanship, and Sister Julia would not have cared if he did have a game to play. "You'll remain until you write your name neatly, Master Abernathy," I could almost hear her say.

This trip to the bleachers resulted in Ernie's 400th home run and a Cubs' victory. It was a fine send-off to school.

1965 Postseason

Time to get excited. One of my favorite all-time non-Chicago teams playing in the World Series. For the second year in a row, a team from the Midwest on TV in October.

Even as a little kid, it seemed to me that this part of the country got overlooked. The NBC Game of the Week, for instance, prepared me for some team in dirty grey uniforms lining up to play the Red Sox in Fenway Park. I became better acquainted with the Green Monster with each passing year; and it seemed that the batting stance of Carl Yastrzemski was imitated so often because it was shown to us so often. Everything from the rubbing of dirt into his hands ("I don't need no stinkin batting gloves") to the positioning of his hands. (It almost looked like Yaz was playing a game to see whose bat could reach the highest when waiting on a pitch. He'd win). So with all this attention to the Red Sox and other eastern teams, I was revved up to see the Minnesota Twins in the Series.

Everywhere you looked on Minnesota's team, you'd find a guy whose baseball card you'd be willing to die for. It started for me with the previously mentioned slugger, Harmon Killebrew. I gush with pride back then when I think about the name of my first Little League team—the Twins—and the position I first played in my first practice— first base. I was the Harmon Killebrew of the league, if you went by team and position, not performance. To rate my baseball heroes from that era, the Killer takes fourth place, trailing only Billy Williams, Ernie Banks, and Frank Howard.

Then the Twins had this cool logo of two guys reaching over a river and shaking hands. I didn't get the geography part back then, so I was clueless that they represented Minneapolis and St. Paul, the Twin Cities. Neither did I comprehend the "T" and "C" on their cap, which also stood for Twin Cities. But it was a neat configuration of the two letters, so what the heck?

Those Twins could have been #4 and #6 in my opinion. A couple of outfielders, one very good and the other borderline Hall-of-Fame material: Bob Allison and Tony Oliva. Allison was big, strong, Anglo, handsome, and good. I throw in the handsome part because I remember him starring in the Aqua-Velva commercials. It was one of those commercials I'd watch intently for the first few seconds because it highlighted one of his homers at home and the scoreboard flashing the distance of the drive. Then it cut to what I think was a camp fire scene showing Bob getting cozy with a member of the opposite sex because he uses Aqua-Velva. This part of the commercial was my cue to check out the contents of our refrigerator.

Oliva, whose real name was Pedro, I believe, hailed from Cuba. I read his story and recall him being poor beyond a poverty we'd ever see in the U.S. In baseball, 200 hits in a season is pretty darn good. Oliva pulled this off as a **rookie.** He was a hitting fool. His stance and style made Yaz look almost orthodox (maybe to be a great hitter back then you'd had to be a lefty who looked funny; think about Oliva, Yaz, and before them a guy called Musial). Tony-O would also have very little clue of the strike zone, practically stand on his tiptoes, throw his bat frequently, and lace ropes all over the field. When I think of Oliva and Killebrew hitting back-to-back, I convinced myself that how can any two consecutive batters, even Ruth and Gehrig, be any better?

There were others: the be-spectacled Rich Rollins at third base; a groovy pitcher with a nickname to match, Mudcat Grant; a dynamite centerfielder who smacked 33 homers as a rookie, Jim Hall; a solid catcher in Earl Battey, a slugging lefty in Don Mincher, and a couple of Jim's who could really pitch: Kaat and Perry (Gaylord's brother). Throw in a shortstop who would win a MVP, Zoilo Versailles, and you had yourself a pretty fair team.

Besides the who, one of the things I liked best about this club was the where. Metropolitan Stadium, in Bloomington, MN was a remarkable place for sports. During the baseball season, a neat looking semi-circle just south of home plate had the word "Twins" inscribed. And way before it was popular, the Twins owned some sort of tracking device that would inform the crowd just how far the recent home run just traveled. However pleasing this site was for baseball, it would be better known for football. The purple-clad Vikings playing play-off football outside in December chills me just thinking about it. Real grass and real cold.

Getting back to baseball, with the names and talent and Midwestern roots of the Twins, how could they lose? Things were looking up after they grabbed a 2-zip lead in the Series by holding serve at home. But then the pitching and defense, mostly pitching, of the LA Dodgers took over. The Twins went oh for three in LA, scoring a grand total of two runs in three games. (It felt like I was watching the White Sox. The Dodger pitching could not be *that* good). The Twins bounced back to win Game 6 at home. Could this be one of those Series where the home team wins every game? Alas, no. I remember hanging at a friend's house and watching Sandy Koufax take down my heroes from the north. Junior Gilliam handled a wicked smash by Killebrew to subdue a threat, and Koufax handled the rest. Koufax pitched on two days rest, tossing a complete game shutout in Game 5. I tried to jinx him by counting the outs as the innings progressed, thinking that a boy watching in Chicago on TV could get into the head of the greatest lefty in my time. It was worth the effort, but nothing could help the Twins that day; Koufax was just too good.

Even though I didn't like the Dodgers, I did admire their style. Scratch out a hit, steal a base, score a run, strike out most of the opposition (Don Drysdale and Koufax combined for 44 K's in that series), and catch the ball should the other team hit it. A very effective way to play, not unlike the '59 White Sox, I'm told (before my time). I learned a big lesson about baseball—if you got one team with great hitting and good pitching, against a team with limited offense but great pitching, put your money on the second team. If the other team doesn't score, you can't lose. Sometimes I think the Cubs just don't get that.

The Twins in their World Series and Dorothy in Oz share a common belief—there's no place like home. In their relatively brief existence, Minnesota has yet to win a World Series game as a visiting team. However, they have been World Champs twice, and came close the other time. How does a team manage to go oh-fer on the road and 11-1 at home? Stats like these are delicious.

1966

This is the year that brought us the incomparable model of the Ford Mustang. BRAZIL '66 was a popular musical group that created a smooth rendition of the BEATLES' song, "Fool on the Hill," among other hits. A major league team relocated as the Milwaukee Braves migrated to Atlanta. Locally, the O'Donnell household moved, too. We left the big city for a western suburb, Hillside. But perhaps the most noteworthy change occurred at the management level: Leo Durocher became the manager for the Cubs, while Eddie Stanky now led the Chisox.

I never saw these two individuals play, but I did see them manage. It's often been said players reflect the personality of their manager. To me, Stanky and Durocher were both serious "old-school" characters. Scrappy, hustling, and hard-nosed are some kinder adjectives that apply to the "Brat" and the "Lip." Durocher, in particular, is not someone likely to be confused with Mother Teresa based on several things I've read from him and about him. But both had an upside that consisted of a strong desire to score one more run than the opposition.

The change on the South Side happened suddenly. The Sox scrapped their way to a lot of wins without a lot of talent. How they competed against teams with far superior skills is a credit to how they played the game and how the game was managed. Stanky was not shy to get into opponents' heads, either. A memorable quote from Stanky on Yaz stands out: "He's an All-Star from the neck down." Ouch. (how can he say that about a guy who went to school, briefly, at Notre Dame?) But maybe this type of attitude helped, because in a couple of years the Sox were right there in a four team pennant race down to the last few games of the season.

Change happened for the Cubs, too, but more gradually. A Durocher line from this era is still replayed. When Leo took over the ball club, he told the media that this was not an 8th place team (their finish in '65). He proved to be a prophet, for in Leo's first year, the Cubs did NOT finish 8th, no way. They finished 10th.

But better times were ahead.

GAMES 7 & 8 June 5, 1966

The radio voice of the White Sox for many years belonged to Bob Elson. His unflappable manner impressed me as a kid. I caught on to a few of his pet phrases, and waited in smiling anticipation for him to use them. For instance, when a third basemen would field a ground ball, I knew that he was about to "peg" it across the infield. In his unassuming style, his way of promoting the game worked. Elson would encourage fans to come to games early to watch players like Killebrew put on a show during batting practice. Another trademark of his was the way he promoted weekend games at Comiskey Park. Mr. Elson would inform the audience that there was a night game on Friday, a day game on Saturday, and a big double-header on Sunday.

Well now here's a kid, not quite nine years old yet, who's about to attend one of those big Sunday double-headers for the first time. If one baseball game is heaven, what superlative can one use to describe two?

A friend of mine from Chicago, Michael Serra, didn't forget about me even though we moved. It was great to be in touch with an old friend (if a third grader can be considered old) in a new environment. He, his dad, and I were about to witness a couple of contests between the Sox and Washington Senators. Back then the Washington Senators were about as competitive as the Washington Generals. (First in peace, first in war, last in the American League was Washington's mantra.) But I'd almost rather see lousy teams to improve the chances of seeing wins for the home team.

Funny what you remember. Being a double-header and looking at the girth of my chum, I knew the concession people were going to be plenty busy. (One lesson in third grade was about compound words. My buddy Michael asked Sister Julia if "fatso" was a compound word. I laughed for five minutes). Now double-headers got special attention in the calendar I had for the Cubs and Sox. I remember that it had two batters present on that date of a DH, not just one. It got pretty crowded if it fell on one of those Sundays at the end of the month where two dates had to share one square. So one would think the key memory would be the two games, and it would be, had it not been for the ice cream I experienced that day. You see, the White Sox had this smooth vanilla ice cream laced with chocolate sauce in a Dixie cup. But that's not all; it also came with this lid that if you pealed it back just so, you could lick the ice cream off it just like the neighbor's puppy dog. And the **best** part was that it came with wooden sticks in this small white paper wrap that the vendor tossed on top of the Dixie cup. When the final tally and memory of the day has been tabulated, the double-header came in second to the sundae on that Sunday.

But the games were fun, too. A respectable 4-1 (there's that score again—I love it) victory by the White Sox in the first game preceded a 12-0 shellacking in the nightcap. Yielding one run in two games is vintage White Sox. But for them to score 12 times in one week, let alone one game, is extraordinary. Twelve White Sox tallies in a game is like twelve mosquito bites in January; it's not impossible, but highly improbable. But if I'm there I'll gladly take it (the runs, not the mosquito bites).

Some background info about the Sox pitching prowess may be helpful: SIX shutouts in a span of ten games—incredible even if you are playing the hapless Senators with frozen baseballs in a park featuring Grand Canyon dimensions. In the four games against the Nats (a nifty abbreviation for Senators), the Sox allowed a grand total of one run. Gary Peters had a no-hitter going into the seventh inning of game 2. This all adds up to an awesome display of pitching domination.

Getting offensive for a moment, the Sox had this pinch-hitter deluxe who resembled a bartender. He looked like one guy you wouldn't want to see in a bathing suit. But he could hit—his name was Smoky Burgess. He played as a catcher for many years in the National League, breaking in with the Cubs in '49 and now finishing up with the Sox. Now throughout my years of watching the Sox play in person, they could claim an organist second to none in wit, talent, and appearance (in my later years I'd have a serious crush on her, this Nancy Faust). She'd belt out the theme of "Andy Griffith" if a player named Andy came up; "You're Sixteen" could be heard if Brian Downing stood at the plate (he wore #16), and Nancy would bang out "Stop in the Name of Love," if the other team was putting together a threatening rally. But she hardly invented wit, for in these pre-Faust days, the organist played, "Don't Let Smoke Get in Your Eyes." Smoky gets all this attention because it was his two-run pinch single that helped the club in the second game rout.

Other performances worthy of mention that day include a slick centerfielder for Chicago named Tommie Agee: 4 for 9 over the two games with 4 runs scored, 5 driven in, and a triple and a tater (cheesy nickname for home run). J.C. Martin, my sister's hero, was a homer shy of hitting for the cycle in the second game. On the other team, Frank Howard, one of my heroes, should have called in sick: 5 whiffs over two games. Another player I remember more for his name rather than performance was Paul Casanova. He had this most unorthodox way of setting up as a catcher—it looked like he was practically sitting on the ground waiting to receive the next pitch. And if you wanted to place goat horns on someone, and who doesn't like doing that, they fit nicely on a Senator infielder called Ken Hamlin. He committed three errors by himself in one game. That's three errors more than the entire Sox team committed over two games. Defense and pitching, or lack thereof, results in a 12-0 score.

Have you ever felt sorry for the other team during a game? I have, and I sometimes still do. There's been so many occasions when this pattern occurs: my team is winning big, I feel sorry for the other guys, and they promptly come back to win and I curse myself for being too nice. If I didn't feel sorry for the other team, they never would have won. Well, **after** this doubleheader I do recall wondering how awful it would be to be a Senators' fan on this day of double defeat. But here comes that pattern—my sympathy toward Washington would return at a later date, indirectly, to bite me. The manager of that Senator team was Gil Hodges, who managed the Miracle Mets of '69.

How good it is to have friends. My dad told me that new ones are like silver and old ones like gold. As the new kid in the neighborhood, friends were a little scarce. This golden oldie of a friend remembered me and brought me to my first double-header. Thanks, Mike, for a great Sunday and sundae, and no, 'fatso' is not a compound word.

GAME 9 July 2, 1966

Quick—what combination of any two things make you think of America? Mom and apple pie? Hot dogs and fireworks? Super Bowls and parties? Politics and corruption? For me, it's the 4th of July and el beisbol; I always thought it fitting to visit a ballpark on or around Independence Day. I might feel this way even if I weren't a baseballaholic. I might come by this honestly through my folks as I scan the archives and notice how many games we attended around this holiday.

In my earliest years of following baseball, the worst teams in the National League were the Mets, Astros, and Cubs. The Senators, Kansas City Athletics, and Boston Red Sox fought to get out of the basement in the Junior Circuit. Of these six teams, the one with a proud tradition of which I was unaware was the Red Sox. Because the first impression is such a lasting one, when I noticed for a few years in the mid-60's that Boston was a bad team, I assumed that they were always a bad team. Second division seemed to be the fate on several clubs, past, present, and future. I had yet to fathom that some teams may just go through dry spells and rebuilding periods (which could last for a century for certain teams that shall remain nameless). So thinking that the Red Sox were lousy, I was confident that this game would end up in the win column.

Sometimes overconfidence can be fatal to managers, players, and fans. This was not one of those times. The Red Sox were bad. How bad? Consider this: Lee Elia homered off a Red Sox pitcher at cavernous Comiskey. Elia is best known for his tirade against Cub fans when he served as Cub manager in the early 80's. Many years prior to his blow-up, which makes me chuckle every time I hear it, Elia was a reserve infielder for both the Cubs and Sox. When Elia goes "yard" against you, it doesn't take a baseball brainiac to know that your pitching is weak.

And this poses an interesting question in a negative vein: until 2000, whose pitching has been worse—the Cubs or the Red Sox? I ask you not to be too quick to answer, but consider the evidence. In 1966, both teams finished dead last in pitching ERA. That's saying something when teams like the Senators and Mets are letting in fewer runs than you are. No doubt that both franchises have boasted individual stars such as Beckett, Maddux, Lonborg, Sutter, Martinez, Prior, Clemens, and Jenkins (who pitched for both), but one would be hard pressed to find a quality *staff* over a two-three year period until the turn of the century. Once quality staffs emerged for the Bosox, so did world championships. Coincidence?

Back to the slugging Elia. After checking the record book, I feel honored. At the tender age of 8, I witnessed Elia's last big league home run. In fact, I saw 1/3 of his major league total that night. But Lee was not one of those high average, low power type of hitters. No sir, not with a .205 lifetime batting average. He would go on to terrorize the National League with a .176 mark with the Cubs. Churning out these numbers, imagine how Jose Santiago, the fairly capable righty on the Red Sox, felt after Elia took him deep in the 2nd inning?

Tommie Agee followed Elia's blast with a homer of his own in the 3rd. For the White Sox, homering in back-to-back innings was a pretty big deal. The scoreboard exploded twice, and I nearly wet my pants in excitement (given the fact that this was a Saturday night with plenty of beer-guzzling Sox fans, I probably was not the only one with bladder issues).

To illustrate how hapless the Boston pitching was that evening consider this fact: they yielded six runs to a White Sox team that had J.C. Martin batting **fifth**! This means there were four players hitting **below** a guy who had 32 career homers and lifetime batting average of .222 over 14 years.

But the Bosox, with hurlers named Osinski and Sadowski and Morehead (who did pitch a no-hitter in '65) followed Santiago with limited success. Joe Horlen was superb in blanking a dangerous lineup featuring Yaz, George Scott, and Reggie Smith (how many remember him breaking in as a second baseman?) Horlen didn't give way to Wilhelm this time; instead he tossed a complete game six hit shutout. He was on his way to a sparkling 2.43 ERA with a final record of 10-13. 10-13?!

Almost as exciting as the exploding scoreboard were the fireworks following the game. For many years this has been huge on the South Side. When I was 8, this was a memorable show: lights, noise, and just the right length. Only one cheesy thing detracted from the experience— the sponsor's logo would somehow works it way into the performance, usually to a chorus of boos. But this was very minor and easily tolerated since the Right Sox won.

GAME 10: July 21, 1966

Studying the games that I attended as a tike, a trend emerges that reveals my folks' competitive nature. It's simply this—seldom would I go to one ballpark with one parent more than two or three times in a row before the other parent would escort me to a game on the other side of town. My best guess is that among other things, I was being recruited to root for her/his team exclusively. Parents are successful in so many ways, but if their goal was to persuade me to choose one team over the other, sorry. I just liked both teams too much to dismiss one or the other. If this was a private battle of baseball allegiance, who was I to get in the way? Determined to stay neutral, I became like the Switzerland of the Chicago baseball wars.

So now it was my mom's turn to take me to Wrigley Field to watch the Cubs play the Reds. This game marked a first—seeing a game from the first-base side of the field. Talk about different perspectives! I got to look right inside the Cubs' dugout. I could now tell if a ball was fair down the left-field line, but clueless on balls hit the other way. The visitors' on-deck circle was much closer, and it was a tad unsettling to be so close to the enemy. On a more positive note, I got to see my hero much closer. The blue #14 on the back of Banks as he effortlessly tossed grounders to his mates prior to each inning was a delightful sight. But the strongest impression from my new vantage point had to be the distance now between home and first base. More on that later.

Getting back to Mr. Cub for a closer look—if ever a ballplayer personified peace, it was he. Not an ounce of cockiness or arrogance, but a ton of self-assuredness. It struck me that I was watching a man truly enjoying himself, and that line of "Let's play two" maybe had some truth to it. Not much over the years has been written or said about Ernie's defense, but in truth I never saw him look clumsy or awkward. I was mesmerized by one piece of equipment, his glove. It fascinated me, how the shape and design of a first baseman's mitt could look so different from all the others. And I remember hearing that he did not have much range at this point in his career, which is why he moved from shortstop to first base. That's an issue that was beyond my understanding when I was nine. But in defense of Ernie's defense, if a ball came his way, he caught it. He might not have been as Graceful as some Cub players at that position, but he was smooth. Watching Ernie lob balls intersecting the diamond was like listening to a Bach instrumental—impossible not to be soothed by it. I never really noticed Banks' classy style until I sat closer to him. Speaking of his class, it's no wonder that he and Durocher did not get along.

As for the distance between home and first, all I could think of was "Wow." Listening to Cub games on the radio, one phrase that stuck with me is that a Cub player was "out by a whisker" at first base. In fact, in the post-Brock years, I can't ever remember a Cub being called safe on a close play at first. Now sitting where I was, I could see why. The distance to first base, combined with a glaring want of speed, made grounders to infielders a hopeless cause.

Now for anyone who has played the game, I ask you this: is it not true that when you as a batter hit the ball into the outfield, the race to first base is a blur? One is aware of time and distance on balls hit on the ground, but this sense of space leaves if the ball is handled by an outfielder. An adrenaline rush, perhaps? It's like this: you hit the ball and then round first. The ninety feet in-between are baseball's version of the Black Hole.

Ignorance is bliss. Had I known how dreadful the Cubs were this year, I might have asked my mom to hold-off on a Wrigley visit for another day/year/century. The Reds weren't good, but the Cubs were far worse. How bad were they? Well, at this date in the season, if the last place Cubs went on an 11 game winning streak, and the next-to-last place Mets went on an 11 game losing streak, the Cubs would still be in last place.

Still, there were things to see—like Ernie keeping loose. Also, some milestones to consider. If 500 and 3000 are magical numbers, then 400 and 2000 can't be that far behind. Our last pilgrimage to the Wrigley Shrine resulted in Ernie's 400th career homer. On this particular day, Ernie would safely hit for the 2001st time. The media didn't make a big deal of things that day because the media AND baseball weren't the big deals back then. But 2001 hits was something the 7,533 watching that game that day appreciated. 2000 hits is like one hit per game for 12 years, not too shabby.

As for our opposition, it should be recorded that this was not the same Cincinnati ball club I saw in '64. The most notable difference or absence was that of Frank Robinson. As Cincy was mired in the middle of the standings, F. Robby was on his way to winning the Triple Crown in the American League. Now baseball wisdom has said on more than one occasion that the best trades are sometimes the ones a team does *not* make. Case in point: Frank Robinson for Milt Pappas. Now Pappas had a fine career, etc... but how do you justify giving up a Frank Robinson? To add salt to the wound, Robinson would play in 4 World Series, winning two of them. To add more salt to more wounds, his team would beat the Reds in the '70 World Series. Meanwhile, Milt Pappas with his consistent yet unspectacular numbers would be traded. Twice. And not make it to the World Series after that exchange for Robinson. Not on a par with the "Brock for Broglio" disaster, but not one that you'd be proud of if you're the Cincinnati general manager.

The other change in the Reds' lineup that caught my eye was their third place hitter: Pete Rose. I wonder how many games Pete played and hit third? It looked strange. And even though this Red team lost Robinson and did not measure up to the Big Red Machine that blitzed through the league years later, this team could score. The batting order featured tough outs in Vada Pinson and Deron Johnson (130 RBI's in 1965). (One other name jumped out at me, the Reds' catcher, Jim Coker. As Herman Franks of the Giants made me hungry, hearing or reading Coker's name made me thirsty).

For a team doing as poorly as the Cubs, this game was a laugher. The 6-1 victory was due mostly to the exploits of Banks (a double, triple, and 2 RBI's) and Don Kessinger (a triple with the bases loaded in the 8th). It was quite a sight to see Mr. Cub scamper to third base on his 35 year-old legs. As he hit third base, and my heart was pounding as quickly as his, I turned to my mom and announced, "Isn't Ernie great?" She agreed.

Another stand-out performance was turned in by another senior citizen, Curt Simmons. The same Curt Simmons who was victimized by Banks' 400th home run was now on the receiving end of Ernie's extra-base hits. He pitched a complete game three-hitter to earn the victory. In case you're wondering, Rose did get one of the three hits for the bad guys. So in 18 innings of watching the Reds play ball in person, they collected a grand total of 4 hits off Cub pitching, and Rose had half of them.

As a footnote to Simmons' performance, I loved it as a kid when a player played well for the Cubs and lousy for other teams. Simmons was a solid pro, but in my book he was OK because he got the loss when he pitched against them, but earned the victory when he pitched for them. For these last two visits to Wrigley Field, Simmons made my day. Think of players who did well for the Cubs and poorly for other teams. Now turn it around—players who underachieved for the Cubs but overall did well for other clubs. Which list is longer? Would the names like Goose Gossage, Dennis Eckersley, Ken Reitz, Mel Rojas, Jeff Blauser, and Nomar Garciaparra come to mind?

Personally, I behold another remarkable stat: of my first 10 games I've seen in person, the Chicago team won nine of them. The Sox took 4 out of 5 (one blemish to the Halos) and the Cubs a perfect 5-0. And keep in mind this was at a time when the Cubs were awful. Sometimes I think this early success distorted my view of Chicago baseball. If I knew then what I know now, I might have quit while I was ahead. But probably not.

GAME 11: August 12, 1966

Revenge. That's how I saw it. Cute. That's how my sister saw it. When it came to baseball, my sister and I operated on different galaxies. As the Chisox took on the Angels, it was a Chance for me to avenge that bitter, and only, setback two years ago. This may not sound very nice, but I truly wanted the home team to beat the hell out of the Angels.

Bravado aside, this game was not going to be easy. The Sox had two things going against them: their own anemic offense and an opposing hurler called Dean Chance. He was the reason my sister brought binoculars to the game. She kept close tabs on him whether he was on the mound, in the dugout, or on his way to the water cooler. Be it scratching, sitting, or spitting, my dad and I got an up-to-the-second report on random Chance happenings. By the way she carried on, you'd think his first name was John, Paul, or Ringo. But it was okay. What the heck, I was at a baseball game; I could put up with almost anything save a second loss to these Californians (no longer the LA Angels, but now the California Angels).

For me, the real Angel attraction stood in left field. Not far from our grandstand seats stood Jimmy Piersall. I memorized the two baseball movies I saw as a kid; I would have memorized more, but those were the only two I saw—<u>Pride of the Yankees</u> and <u>Fear Strikes Out</u>. Now you don't have to be a baseball junkie to appreciate Gary Cooper's famous line, "Today, I consider myself ..." Yet for my fourth grade money, which amounted to a nickel per week, right next to Gary Cooper I'd put Tony Perkins, who captivated me as a crazy with baseball cleats. Who could forget the scene where Perkins, as a young Jimmy Piersall, was playing catch with his psycho dad, Karl Malden, and tears started streaking down young Jimmy's cheeks. I asked my dad why the boy was crying, and he told me that when you caught a baseball thrown hard, it could really hurt. I found out through experience that he was really right.

And then there was the scariest Perkins' scene in his career that did not involve Janet Leigh. It was the part where Jimmy belts an inside-the-park homer and upon scoring he proceeds to climb the screen behind home plate. Classic stuff. Turning back to baseball reality, I was a bit dumbfounded to think that the protagonist of this film was shouting distance from us in left field. I shan't forget what the real Piersall was doing that night—talking with fans perched above the left field wall, eating peanuts that they tossed down to him, and playing with his shirt tail untucked. How could you not be drawn to this guy? He was more entertaining than the game, and I started to wonder if I'd get to see a player climb a fence in person. As a matter of fact, Piersall put me in another tough position. I wanted to see the Sox win, of course, but I also wanted to see Jimmy do well.

Both came true! Piersall got a hit (and by the end of his career, that qualified as a good game) and the Sox demolished the Angels, 1-0. If it weren't for Chicago's main weapon, the wild pitch, they still might be playing some 40 years later. The White Sox offensive rampage went like this: a single by Pete Ward in the 5th inning, a ground-out to advance him, and two wild pitches. Just enough. Against the Angels, you die by the passed ball and live by the wild pitch. No matter, a win by default is still a win as the Sox got one more person to cross home than the Angels did.

Does good pitching handle good hitting? Evidently, and Sox fans historically hope so. Could you imagine a pep talk by Manager Stanky, "OK guys, just don't let them score and we'll get 'em when their pitcher throws a couple to the screen." In fairness, to reduce the Sox success to good pitching and luck does not do the team justice. Even as a kid, I saw that the Sox just seemed to know what they were doing on the field. As that baseball guru Clint Eastwood might say, "A team has to know its limitations," and the Sox were well aware of the things they couldn't do on offense. So it looked to me that they put their focus on defense. Unlike the team on the North Side, defense was not an after thought, nor was it something to be endured until we could smack some homers again. No, this Sox team had the fielders who could run and catch the ball. People like Jim Landis, Ken Berry, and Tommie Agee were superb. Sox infielders of this era were also solid—Al Weis couldn't hit his kid's weight, but his hands were sure. And Tommie McCraw at first was more than adequate. This combination of pitching well and catching the ball once it was hit brought many more victories to the Sox as opposed to the Cubs' emphasis on offense.

This 1-0 decision must have been a tough loss to swallow for my sister's heart-throb (she was way past J.C. Martin by then). Imagine giving up five total bases over the course of an entire game and losing! But my sister Jean didn't care too much about the trivial things like who wins and loses. The two hour game was fine with her as those binoculars started getting heavy.

(Speaking of heart-throbs, the low attendance figure for that hot August night was due to, some say, an attraction going on in some other part of town that evening. For $5.00 you could watch some band from Liverpool, England perform. I believe it was at the Chicago Amphitheater. I wonder if that group ever made it).

The winning pitcher that night is one of the best ever NOT to be in the Hall-of-Fame, Tommy John. After this four-hit shutout, his record stood at 11-6 with and ERA of 2.25. As a sign of the times, reports suggest that his record would be much better had he not missed much time serving for the Indiana National Guard.

No post-game ice cream on an airplane was needed that night. I got my revenge, and victory was sweet enough. But I do recall food playing a role in the evening's affairs. The usual consumption of hot dogs wouldn't happen at this game because it was a Friday. In 1966, veggie things were pretty much unheard of, and you can only ingest so much popcorn and peanuts before a parent starts looking for some semblance of nutrition. What's a Catholic to do?

So my dad leaves me in the care of my big sister, whose eyes are glued to the Angelic pitcher, as papa bear hunts for food under the third base seats. He returns with cheese sandwiches. On white bread. With no mayonnaise. And not grilled. Perfect. To my Irish-Catholic taste, watching a baseball game with people he loved on a Friday night, this was a culinary feast. Thanks dad.

POST-SEASON 1966

Final tally for this year: Chicago teams 5, Bad guys 0. Not bad for two teams that finished a combined 142-182. Of course, the Cubs had the lion share of defeats—103 to be precise (no Cub team has lost more since). This reveals that either my folks knew how to pick the right games to go to, or we were just plain lucky. Maybe it was a combination of both.

League leaders at season's end indicated a definite void of White Sox regulars, save one, Tommie Agee. In the AL, Agee placed third in stolen bases with 44 (Campaneris of the A's led with 52, followed by Buford's 51). Agee rapped 172 hits to finish 4th in that category, he wound up 4th in total bases, and only two players in the league scored more runs—F. Robinson and Tony Oliva. You may or may not know where I'm going with this: on a team so lacking in offense, why did the Sox trade a premium offensive player? Couldn't the Sox see that Agee was destined for stardom? And more importantly, couldn't they foresee that he would break Cubs' hearts in 1969? (Come to think of it, maybe the Sox could see that Agee would mess up the Cubs, so they traded him to the Mets. Perhaps they regret not trading him sooner).

Given these numbers, Agee would go on to play only one more season for the Sox. In fairness to White Sox brass, Agee's offensive output took a big hit in '67. In fairness to Agee, almost everyone's output took a big hit in '67, the year of the pitcher. Obviously, it came down to value and who the Sox could get in return. So here's who the Sox got in return for Agee and Al Weis: Tommie Davis, Jack Fisher, Billy Wynne, and Buddy Booker. Buddy Booker?! The key was Davis. I remember him for several things: being the brother of Willie Davis (the Dodger, not the Packer), driving in a boatload of runs one season, and badly breaking his leg. I assume the Sox acquired him for that second reason. In retrospect, it wasn't the world's worst trade. Agee did NOT have a Lou Brock type of career, but he did do a great Superman impersonation in the '69 Series, did he not? And Agee was traded twice more after the Mets, to the Astros and Cardinals. But one still has to wonder. What is baseball if not for second-guessing?

The 1966 World Series was a match between two classy organizations: the Dodgers and the Orioles. The O's had some power with the likes of Boog Powell and the two Robinsons. But by and large, both teams relied on pitching and defense. Big surprise. Watching teams like this in the post-season was both exciting and frustrating to me as a fourth-grader. Exciting because the play was so good, frustrating because it showed how far away the Chicago teams were from this caliber of baseball.

I must confess that I had my coping techniques long before people talked about coping techniques. That is this: while I loved the local teams, I had to pick out other teams to like in order to be involved in things like the World Series. I had to be involved in the biggest games, and I knew Chicago wasn't going to be there.

So this year I rooted for the Orioles. This series gave me some satisfaction after the Twinkies demise in '65. Here's an incredible stat about the '66 Series: after the third inning of Game 1, the Dodgers would not score a run again until 1967. That's 33 innings of offensive futility. Maybe they hired the White Sox hitting instructor.

Of course, credit has to go to those pitchers who wore the emblem of the cocky bird. Moe Drabowsky shut down LA in the first game, and then Jim Palmer, Wally Bunker, and Dave McNally all threw shutouts. There was one other amazing feature in this one-sided affair—Willie Davis (brother of Tommie) committed three errors in one inning; in fact, I believe the errors were on the *same play*. I doubt if that's ever been duplicated. But it hardly mattered; can't win if you don't score.

Now guess who was pitching at the time of the Davis fiasco? None other than Sandy Koufax. I wonder how many people knew that this would be Koufax's very last performance in the major leagues. To close the books on Sandy's career, consider this bit of Koufax trivia that falls under the category of Life Isn't Fair: in 57 innings of World Series competition, Sandy posted a 0.95 ERA. Yet he still managed to lose 3 games.

PRESEASON: 1967

It was the best of times. A pack of baseball cards cost you a nickel. Calculate the return on your investment if one of those five cards happened to be Nolan Ryan's rookie card. If you were to tell one of us who collected these cards that they someday might be valued at over $1,000.00, we'd probably come back at you with, "Sure, and one day a guy will walk on the moon." It's mind-boggling to think that a Mickey Mantle card or a Ryan rookie card could have so much value when they could have easily been inserted in a bicycle's tire spokes. The checklists, the team pictures, and the rookie cards were the most likely candidates for the spokes. Think the unthinkable: a kid trashing the card of Nolan Ryan while cramming that pungent pink bubble-gum into his mouth. (Some days that gum was stale and cracked in two; other times it was just right and as pliable as play-dough). How many thousands of dollars in cards were thrown away or trashed in a bike? The world may never know, and maybe that's not such a bad thing.

Fortunately, I hung on to my cards. Tom, a friend who lived across the street, and I had this game where we used our baseball cards. And naturally, the better your cards, the better your chances of winning. This game saved me because it gave me reason to keep these cards in fairly decent condition. But still, I would have guessed that the Cubs and Sox would have won dozens of world championships before these cards had any value. Only in America could one card from one pack help you pay for someone's college education.

This year also marked my first crack at Little League. The highlight of this experience was our team—the Twins—celebrating a win, loss, or tie at the local A & W after the game. The creamy root beer quenched our thirst, but we weren't satisfied just yet. Some of us would grab a handful of these impossible-to-open catsup packets and strategically align them on the ground by unsuspecting teammates. Then we'd jump on them with all our Little League might, getting the contents to squirt high and deep into the twilight air. Seeing the red blend in with Little League attire resulted in squeals of delight from kids, but angry looks from coaches, parents, and A & W management.

On nights I wasn't playing, I'd wolf down a dinner, dry the dishes, and rush to the nearby deli to grab a coke and an ice cream sandwich for a quarter. Fresh from this sugar-high, I'd pop a few wheelies on my Stingray bike, then head over to watch the older kids in Pony League play ball. There were worse ways to live.

Pick-up games with hard balls, whiffle balls, rubber balls, softballs, etc. dominated our waking hours. The size of the playing field determined the type of ball we used. Bikes served as the main and sometimes the sole means of transportation. The Beatles were still going strong, and I was too young to be affected by the Vietnam War and civil unrest. Too young to work, but money never seemed to be an issue. I was old enough for a lot of the good things, and too young for a lot of the ugliness. Fun was plentiful, and responsibilities were scarce. The Cubs were improving, and the Sox were pennant contenders. It truly was the best of times.

GAME 12: April 8, 1967

How confident are you that the team for which you're rooting will win that day? Now if you're a Chicago baseball fan, be honest, how often have you gone to the ballpark just knowing that the your team is a lock? It was my first "game" of 1967, and I was *guaranteed* a happy outcome. The Cubs were playing the Sox in an exhibition game at Wrigley Field.

Attending a ballgame in the Midwest prior to Memorial Day is risky business. Raw wind, rain, and cold are what you can expect on a good day. This day would be no different. Whatever the weather today, with inter-league play a Cubs-Sox game is hyped ad nauseam and the game is an automatic sell-out weeks in advance. Not so in 1967—a gate of 10,893 attests to that.

Going to the ballpark with my mom AND dad was an unusual experience. My mom's favorite place was not Comiskey Park. For my dad, a trip to Wrigley Field was about as pleasant as having molars drilled. One day when we were much older we had a surprise planned for my dad in the big city. When we vaguely informed him of this trip, he asked in a most forlorn voice, "Will it hurt?" We chuckled because we knew exactly what he meant. Surprisingly, we weren't going to Wrigley Field this time, so anything else would be most welcome in his book.

But every so often my folks would abandon their comfort zone and cross Chicago's Mason-Dixon line (Madison Avenue) to humor someone in the family, usually me. We bundled up that day and took in the game from the deep grandstands at Wrigley, where wind-chill factors can resemble temperatures found on Groundhog's Day. The weather condition was secondary, however. My real dilemma was this: one of my parents was not going to be happy with the outcome of this game. In the back of my mind, I was worried about an inevitable disappointment on her or his behalf. I was starting to think this was a bad idea.

Hindsight tells me that few people are as nuts as I am, including my folks. Sure, my parents would rather see their team win than lose, but a defeat to them never seemed to sting them as much as it stung me. I think they had a healthier view and a better handle on things. Come to think of it, outside of Notre Dame football, passion seldom surfaced in the world of sports for my mom and dad.

This sloppy exhibition game dragged on and on. You know it wasn't the real thing when you examine the Sox offensive numbers: 16 hits, 5 doubles, 1 homer. Now before even the most optimistic Sox fan rejoiced in this output, their mood would be sobered when they considered the quality of the opposing pitching. But even weirder than the Sox offense was the Sox defense: they committed four errors. Four errors by the White Sox??!! Four hits in one game, sure, but four errors in one game?! Quite an exhibition, indeed. The Sox did not come close to committing four errors in all the games I saw them play between 1964 and 1966.

Aside from this totally out-of-character performance by the White Sox, the game provided a few pearls:

- A Cub named Norm Gigon hit a pinch homer off Gary Peters.
- My brother's favorite player, Gerry McNertney, singled and doubled.
- The fab five at the top of the Cubs' lineup (you know who they are) all hit safely.

But what I vividly recall in this lackluster game was the batting stance of a player the Cubs recently acquired. His name was Lee Thomas, and I was mesmerized by his wide open batting stance. The only thing I ever saw remotely like it belonged to the second basemen on Detroit, Dick McAuliffe. I couldn't wait to get home to start imitating it in our backyard whiffle ball games. It also didn't hurt that he was a good guy to have on the bench, so said my dad. Never hearing of him, but seeing his stance, I heartily agreed.

Now the Sox had a player who made an even greater impression on me. His name was Walt Williams. Here's a summary of what the Sox had in him:

1. He got lost on his way to Wrigley Field (I can relate—happened to me several times when I first started driving).

2. He banged out two doubles and a single as a lead-off man, albeit against Cub pitching.

3. He had a head that rested on shoulders with no neck in between.

4. He possessed a very cool autograph—the "W" is written just once with the "alt" and the "illiams" standing next to the "W" as bunk beds.

5.   He smiled a lot.

6.   He pounded his glove several times before catching a fly ball.

7.   He had a zest for life that was contagious.

In short, and Williams was short, this guy was the poster player for fan clubs. Consider him a poor man's Ernie Banks in popularity; a true delight and ambassador for his team. Cub fans had to like him just like Sox fans had to like Ernie.

GAME 13: June 26, 1967

Right around the year 2000, I posed a question to a big league ballplayer that I had wondered about since I was a kid. It was this: If a fan wants to maximize his chances of witnessing a win for the team for which he's rooting, is it better to attend a game after a victory or after a defeat? To elaborate, does the team suffer from complacency after a win, or do they have that nebulous thing called momentum to improve their odds? And, after a loss, will a team be more determined or more deflated? I posed this question to Mickey Morandini, the one time second baseman for the Cubs and one of the few players to record an unassisted triple play, the rarest feat in the game.

Morandini's response, "The better chance for victory comes after a win, especially if it is a day game following a night game. It just seems that momentum rolls into the next day. And show up the day Kerry Wood is pitching." (Note: Morandini's comments about Wood were made prior to his seemingly perpetual placement on the disabled list as a starting pitcher).

This game in late June would challenge the Morandini theory. (Keep in mind that Morandini was not yet in pre-school when this game was played). The Cubs were riding a seven game winning streak and were playing another team of Morandini's, the Philadelphia Phillies. Something was slightly awry at our household: we were supposed to attend the Ladies' Day game on Thursday, but ended up spectating the Senior Citizens' matinee on Tuesday (at that time they were all matinees, of course). A bad omen, perhaps? Aside from more gray hair and fewer high-pitched voices, I didn't notice too many things that were different. But I held out hope that momentum would carry the day over the Vance Law of Averages.

To see a team that I had yet to see in person, like the Phillies, provided me with ample things to observe. The first noticeable thing after a lengthy absence had nothing to do with the Phils. I was caught up again in the abundance of green as I walked up those stairs. Remember we were still 1–2 years away from colored TV, and newspapers were virtually always in black and white. The second thing that caught my eye was the scoreboard. Once again the Cubs were playing a team with way too many letters; it was flat-out intimidating. How could my heroes with their puny four letters outscore a team with too many letters to count? It just didn't seem fair. I also thought that this had to be a fire hazard or safety issue of some kind: isn't it dangerous to have all those letters crammed into a tiny space. Wouldn't the scoreboard explode or implode the way a suitcase might after a return home with too many souvenirs?

Attention then shifts to the enemy. The color of the Phillies' uniforms would provide a pleasant contrast to Cub blue. The Philly red may not have been as vivid as the Cincinnati or St. Louis uniform, but it sure looked a lot better than whatever you got on a black and white telecast. Most memorable of the Phils' attire were the numerals on the back. Whereas the Cubs and most teams had numerals (few had names) that were modest in length, the Phillies' numerals began at the bottom of their neck and concluded just north of their posterior, I kid you not. I thought this as some sort of oversight, "Excuse me, Mr. Callison, but your numbers are too long. Mr. Allen, is it hard running around the bases because your numbers are so big?" What about names on jerseys? I felt they were unnecessary. What fan did not know that Cookie Rojas wore glasses. Or that Richie Allen carried himself like Shaft before there was a Shaft, "Who's the cat that won't strike out when there's base runners all about ..." Getting back to the enormous numbers, the red "6" on the back of Johnny Callison's covered most of his body. So not only was there no need for names, there was no place for them.

The teams that had names on the back were the exception. Clubs like the Reds, Redbirds, White Sox and Orioles come to mind. I recall that some teams placed names only on the home jersey. But true fans needed no stinkin names. Could you imagine someone exclaiming, "Oh, who is that number "21" on the Pirates?" or, "that # 7 on the Yankees looks like a player." Numerals debuted on baseball jerseys to identify spots in the batting order. I'm glad this practice changed: I'd hate to see Billy batting 26th and Durocher leading off! Still, if you managed the Yanks, wouldn't you be tempted to issue # 3 to Gehrig and # 4 to Ruth?

On this particular day the villain of our story was not a name player. Rather, it was a blue-collar, capable player with a simple name, Don Lock. Lock, I believe, wore a gigantic '24' on his back, and delivered a 3-run bomb in the third inning. Now would you be worried if you trailed by two runs in the early innings of a game at Wrigley Field? What are the chances that a 3-1 lead would hold up?

Hardly a Lock, especially when the opposing pitcher has a record of 1-5 (Rick Wise). Add this to the mix: Kessinger owned a 10 game hitting streak, while Santo's stood at 12. And if they didn't produce surely Beckert, Williams, Banks, etc. would come through.

Not today. Hats off to the Phillies manager; it was Wise to pitch Rick. He pitched effectively into the 7th (not a complete game, but what is termed a "quality start" today), and he ended the Cubs winning streak with a 4-2 victory.

Even though Wise pitched well (more on him later), the bullpens impressed me the most. The Cub relief corps epitomized contrast. After the starter Curt Simmons departed in the 4th (by some odd coincidence he started the last three games I saw at Wrigley Field, for 2 different clubs), Leo Durocher brought in Dick Radatz, AKA **the Monster.** Radatz achieved fame for the Bosox, but also pitched well in a short stint with the Cubs. He lasted until the 8th, at which point Chuck Hartenstein, AKA **Twiggy,** took over. I'd be willing to bet that two Hartensteins could fit into one Radatz uniform. I'd also go double or nothing that the Phillies numerals were longer than Twiggy. Size doesn't always matter, as both relievers shut down the Phillies on just one hit over the last five innings.

Unfortunately, the *short* and *long* relief pitching for the Cubs was in vain. Wise's relief help was also good, in the form of Dick Hall. Hall's style was herky-jerky. With his 6'6" frame, a lot of motion would come at the batter, and then a slight pause. Kind of like that slight pause at the top of a roller coaster—you know something is coming at you quickly, so let's get on with it. Anyway, Hall's delivery must have thrown off the timing of the Cub hitters that day. Hall's save was legit: 2 1/3 of innings pitched with the tying runs on base; now that's a save.

It looked like the Cubs would pull this out in the end, especially with the way they had been playing and given Morandini's theory on momentum. But it was not to be, so a young boy and a bunch of senior citizens left the ballpark disappointed. And to top it off, guess what happened on the Ladies Day game that we were supposed to attend? That's right, the Cubs beat Pittsburgh. Ouch. Nothing against senior citizens, but I learned my lesson that day. Go on the day you're supposed to go, Ladies Day with mom, and don't mess things up. And above all else, don't be superstitious.

A few more comments on the winning pitcher, Rick Wise. Years ago I visited with him as he served as a pitching coach for a Class A minor league team in the Midwest League. I doubt if more than twenty people in the stadium that night knew anything about Rick Wise. But I did, and we had a pleasant conversation. Actually, it was more like I asked, he talked, and I listened.

This is what I learned, Rick Wise ...

- Likes Fergie Jenkins, an old teammate
- Has the longest fingers I have ever seen
- Says that the best pitch to throw is a fastball that "has an idea to go with it."
- Threw a no-hitter
- Homered twice in the game that he threw a no-hitter (did you think anyone else ever homered twice and threw a no-hitter in the same game, at any level of baseball from the majors down to backyard whiffle?)
- Drinks hot coffee on a warm summer night
- Was traded for Steve Carlton, straight up.
- Is a prankster—he feinted as though he was going to drop my ball signed by Bob Feller in a mud puddle.

- Was the winning pitcher in the most memorable game in my lifetime.

Any guess what that game might be? I'll give you a two-word clue and I'm sure you'll get it: Carlton Fisk. Yep, it surprised me too. Game 6 of the 1975 World Series. As Fisk uses all the pudgy body language he can muster to keep his drive fair, Rick Wise gets the credit for the win in that epic battle. I bet the average fan does not know that.

Perusing the list of the probable starting pitchers in the sports section of the CHICAGO TRIBUNE on June 27, 1967, I noticed something that would fall somewhere between trivial and unbelievable–in each city where a National League game was being played, a Hall-of-Fame pitcher was scheduled to pitch. Here they are: Fergie Jenkins in Chicago, Tom Seaver in New York, Phil Niekro in Atlanta, Juan Marichal in St. Louis, and Don Drysdale in Cincinnati. I've got to wonder how often something like that occurs? It was indeed the best of times for a kid growing up in 1967.

GAME 14: August 10, 1967

I grew up in a time and place when justice and getting even was a priority. Obviously, this value carried over into watching baseball games for the very next game I attended starred the same two teams at the same ballpark only a couple of months later. Would it be the same outcome? On the Phillies' next trip through Chicago two significant differences were in the mix since the June contest: 1) the Phils were on an eight-game win streak 2) my mom was taking us on *Ladies' Day*, not Senior Citizens' Day. While justice and winning streaks are important, they're trumped by superstition.

Looking back at the original schedule, more comparisons can be drawn between then and now. Initially August 10 was supposed to be an off-day. My guess is that a rain out occurred earlier in the season, making this a five-game series starting on a Thursday and concluding with a Sunday doubleheader. Speaking of doubleheaders, the Cubs had **four** scheduled at home in a span of one month. That's not taking into account doubleheaders on the road, which were common fare for Sundays. Now I'd be surprised if the Cubs played four twin-bills in the span of two seasons, let alone one month. Not only are double-headers rapidly approaching extinction, but they are now becoming a day/night affair which clears the crowd after the first game so the second gate won't be lost. $o it look$ like thing$ have changed.

Examining box scores from two teams playing each other six weeks apart can yield tendencies about managers, right-lefty match-ups, and player personnel. For instance, key hitters of the Phillie lineup stayed intact: Billy Cowan and Allen as the 2 and 4 hitters. Don Lock and Gene Oliver flip-flopped in the batting order, making me think that Oliver is hitting slightly better than Lock at this point. The third biggest change is a break for the Cubs—Johnny Callison was not in the starting lineup. I still remember him walloping a late-inning homer in the '64 All-Star game to give the NL a dramatic win. The second biggest change is at first base. In June, Tony Taylor played that position and lead-off. (Certain positions just don't seem like lead-off positions: C, 3B, and 1B, but oh well). In August, Bill White was playing first base. Now Bill White was a very fine player in the peak of his career, knocking in 100 runs four different times. He ended up with a lifetime average of .286 at a time when pitching was solid. But I noticed that his playing time and his numbers dropped drastically in '67, suggesting an injury and/or age matters. Nevertheless, to see White not playing in June and later playing but batting seventh, behind guys like Don Lock and Gene Oliver, surprised me, even if a lefty was starting for the Cubs both times (Curt Simmons and Rob Gardner).

Now the biggest change in the Phillie lineup is the pitcher. Someone said momentum is as good as the next day's starting pitcher, and that being the case, the winning streak of the Phils is as good as Larry Jackson. Now along with justice and superstition, loyalty matters. Rooting against a guy who gave me my first thrill as a baseball spectator with a near perfect game challenged me, but not for long. Sorry, Larry, better luck in your next start, and maybe a "No Decision" in this one.

The Cub lineup stayed pretty much intact as well. Practically anyone in Chicago could rattle off the first five Cub hitters from this era, most likely in a voice imitating Pat Pieper, the PA announcer. Kessinger SS, Beckert 2B, Williams LF, Santo 3B, Banks 1B, then who? Names like Hickman, Hundley, Pepitone, Phillips, etc. would find homes toward the latter part of the lineup. The infield and catcher positions were set, but the other two outfield positions next to Williams had a transitory feel to them. For instance, Ted Savage and Al Spangler started in June (CF and RF, respectively) but Adolfo Phillips and Cleo James got the nod in August. In both games, the pitcher emerged from deep in the rotation; indeed, if even in the rotation at all. You recall that Curt Simmons started in June, and now Rob Gardner took the hill in August. Both were lefties, and both didn't last long with the Cubs, but both pitched well when I was there.

Now much has been said about the Friendly Confines being a launching pad. There's no denying that **provided** that the wind is blowing out. But when the wind blows in, as it does more often than not, and the grass grows tall, hitting there can be quite a challenge. It was this day as winds howled in from center field at over 20 miles per hour.

"He who scores first usually wins." I think someone once said that. I hoped that would be true today, as three singles and a sac. fly by Santo put the Cubs up 2 nil. But my old friend Larry Jackson and my new friend Rob Gardner, with the wind at their backs, put up goose eggs through six innings after the tallies in the first.

Now it was up to the bullpens. Here are some names you've seen before: Dick Hall and Chuck Hartnestein. In painful fashion, the Phils pulled even with singletons in the 7th and 8th frames. How it hurts to be ahead for a couple hours or so and suddenly not be winning. Now we had ourselves a game, 2-2 in the bottom of the eighth. It seems the bottom of the 8th is critical and sometimes flies under the radar. Everyone knows that the game is often determined with any scoring from the 9th inning on, but to go ahead in the bottom of the 8th is so important because then the task is simplified—if we get three outs before they score, we win. I'm intrigued and attracted to sports when it can be broken down like that.

With that great build-up, I'm sure you're not expecting a 1-2-3 eighth, are you? Thanks to the wind, Cubs fans had something to cheer about again (remember, they haven't scored since the 1st. So when the Phils tie up the game, you no longer have enough runs to win but have to overcome inertia on offense and score). Anyway, a colorful, talented and inconsistent performer named Adolfo Phillips hits one to left. The new left fielder is Johnny Briggs, and his forte is offense, not defense. Well, Briggs wrestles with the wind-blown ball and loses. His miscue allows Phillips to reach second base. A couple of one-out singles by Kessinger and Beckert give the Cubs the lead again. Guarded optimism reigns as the game enters the 9th.

"Twiggy" Hartenstein couldn't hold the lead for Gardner, but now he's got a chance to win if the next Cub reliever does his job. His name is Bill Stoneman. Years before employment as the GM for the Angels, Bill Stoneman threw a no-hitter for the Montreal Expos. And before he did that, he spent some with the Cubs. On this day, he was perfect.

I remember Bill White batting with one out in the 9th and popping out to Banks at first. For the first time that day I relaxed and felt a rush of relief when Ernie caught the ball. One fly ball later to Billy Williams, and victory was ours. A hard-fought 3-2 victory over the Phils and Dick Hall, no less, who gave up that unearned run in the 8th. (So another hope of mine, that my old pal Larry Jackson would not lose, came to fruition. His team did fall short, which is good, but he wasn't the losing pitcher. Hooray).

With this win, it meant that both teams that I saw beat Chicago (the Angels and Phillies) had now lost to our heroes as well. Getting even is sweet.

GAMES 15 & 16: August 22, 1967

During the school year, my mom's morning routine consisted of getting her children out of bed (no small feat), fixing us breakfast, and coaxing us into some sort of readiness for the day ahead. All this was done to the background chatter of Wally Phillips, who had a pretty popular morning radio program. Now this was the same station, oddly enough, which broadcast the Cubs, WGN. In fact, I recall a fair amount of razzing that took place between the Cub broadcasters and Mr. Phillips. Imagine watching a game and the cameras cut away to a scene that showed one person surrounded by scores of empty seats (not uncommon). The Cub announcers might mention that Wally Phillips has his fan club in full force at the ball game today. Stuff like that could amuse the audience if the game was less than thrilling.

One morning my mom woke me from my stupor with a radio to my ear playing one of my favorite songs at that time, "King of the Road" by Roger Miller. Evidently my mom called Wally and asked if he would play this song, and he obliged. Another practice of Wally's that no doubt endeared his listeners included the frequent dishing out of freebies to certain callers. Very common today, but probably a bigger deal back then. On the morning of August 22, my mom happened to be a lucky listener who scored two tickets to a White Sox game. But it gets better: a twi-night double header against the Yankees with Mickey Mantle still playing. I might have missed out on Willie Mays, but I was going to see Mickey Mantle. Without a doubt, I'd rather have that ticket in my hand than the winning ticket for the 6 million dollar lottery.

So many things stand out. First, and perhaps most delightfully, the Yankees were awful. Sometimes I think baseball is popular because it gives so many people across the country a chance to hate the Yankees. I wonder if that constant will ever change. How bad were the Yanks? They occupied the second-to-last position in the standings (only the Kansas City *Athletics* looked up to them). Still only nine, I was learning an important truth: watching a hated team lose can be more enjoyable than watching beloved teams win. It's not something of which I'm proud, but there's no sense denying it.

This twilight affair nearly burst with irony, for it was definitely the twilight of Mantle's career. No matter how much I hated the Yankees, a part of me was melancholy to witness the doleful deterioration of Mickey's greatness.

I cherish the memory—at Comiskey Park, mind you—of viewing a huge white banner unfurled in the left field lower deck grandstands with nothing but an enormous, black #7. This happened right as Mantle was introduced for the first time as he strolled to the batter's box. My dad had to point it out to me because I was too enamored with my scorekeeping duties to notice.

Then I sensed something significant was occurring, Sox fans never paid homage to the opposition in this fashion, at least not in any way that I could remember. The simple banner was a bit ominous, too, for Mickey happened to be batting righty against the southpaw offerings of Chisox hurler, Wilbur Wood. Should Mantle connect against a knuckler that didn't knuckle, I could envision the ball making toward that sign like a comet. "OK," I thought, "that's a nice gesture but we can take it down now. Let's not give Mr. Mantle any ideas." (If you ever watched the movie JAWS 2, there's a scene where the mother screams at her children to get out of the water after she sees in a book what damage the great white shark can inflict. That's how I felt about this banner).

Discussion of Mantle's prowess in all aspects of the game would be redundant and unnecessary. To have that much power and speed contained in one athlete almost doesn't seem fair. But the legendary defending of the outfield would have to stay legendary for me, because on this evening Mickey was relegated to first base. Yankee management tried to squeeze as much out of the man's abused body as possible, and first base was the best option in the days prior to the designated hitter. But better that than nothing, which is what happened in the second game as Mantle sat that one out.

But legendary ballplayers could be found in both dugouts that night. White Sox brass picked up a couple greats of their own hoping their leadership, if not their skill, would lead this meek club to a pennant. Ken Boyer, the great Cardinal third basemen and 1964 MVP now played with the Pale Hose. Simply a solid, unassuming professional. And then there was a new right fielder: Rocco Dominico Colavito. My friend across the street and I would say his entire name at times, always resulting in giggles and snorts. Rocky Colavito, one of those players you'd love to have in your pack of baseball cards, was now property of the White Sox. Wow. These two guys might have been on the way out, but they added a presence in the middle of the lineup that demanded instant respect. Mantle, Boyer, and Colavito—three greats that I got to see up close and personal. No beef here if they were past their prime.

Perched in our seats courtesy of Mr. Phillips, I revisit several moments of glee. One was a throw by Rocky Colavito. It was somewhere in the middle innings of a close game. A Yankee runner and third base coach were rash enough to test Mr. Colavito's arm. I could almost hear Dirty Harry snarl: "Go ahead, make my day."

Now hockey has its penalty shot, football its last second field goal attempt, and basketball has buzzer-beaters galore. But for my money, the most exciting play to watch is a man with speed tagging up from third as an outfielder with a strong arm in the medium deep outfield is poised to catch the ball. Sport at its finest. Now when the dust settled and Colavito had another notch in his assist holster, what impressed me more than the throw was my old man's reaction. His words, **"Did you see that throw???!!!"** were spoken with the same fervor and intensity as when Notre Dame scored a late touchdown to take the lead against a formidable opponent. I seldom, if ever, heard my dad get that excited over baseball. A big fan of the Sox, yes, but nowhere near the passion of the Fighting Irish and college football. So hearing that voice used only for Saturdays in the fall alerted me that something very special just transpired.

The other moment to lock away came in the top of the ninth. It was that classic situation that you and your buddies played out hundreds of times in the backyard, only this time it was real. You know how the litany goes: top of the ninth, two outs, bases loaded, and the visiting team trails by one run. Don McMahon called in from the bullpen (I don't recall if he got a lift from that nifty golf cart, or if he jogged, or if he walked to the mound, but that trip had to be stressful for him. By this time I was out of fingernails). It was that time of game when one eye is on your scorecard and the other eye on the dugout to see who might emerge as a pinch-hitter. My dad was dreading the appearance of Joe Pepitone. When my dad saw it wasn't Pepi, he exclaimed, "Wow, he must really be in the doghouse." To be honest I wasn't familiar with that expression, but I figured that the doghouse must be somewhat akin to the outhouse. Anyway, the leadoff man for the Yankees, Horace Clarke, was going to bat. Now just when you think the situation can't hold any more drama, it gets more dramatic. McMahon and Clarke battle to a full count. Now the outcome of the game is riding on the next pitch. No biggie. (How can I burst into tears when there's another game to be played? I'll get my other scorecard wet). Anyway, McMahon gives it the full country-type windup, reaches back for something extra, and unloads a fastball that's traveling toward the upper, upper end of the Frank Howard strike zone (translation: it's a foot over Clarke's head). But wait, the batter swung, and ... and .... And ..... he missed!!! Somewhere the Mormon Tabernacle Choir breaks into several rounds of **Alleluia.** Sox defeat the hated Yankees, 3-2, as Clarke struck out on a pitch that had tie written all over it. I yelled, cheered, screamed, and carried on for pretty much the duration between games of the double-header. After the whiff, my dad's voice approached that Notre Dame pitch again. Thank you mom, dad, Wally Phillips, Rocky Colavito, Don McMahon, and Horace Clarke.

I'd like to report that the second game surpassed the first in drama, excitement, and level of play, but if I did that, my nose would put Pinocchio's to shame. This game looked like a mismatch from the get-go. Look at the starting pitchers: for the White Sox, Joe Horlen with a record of 14-3; for the Yankees, Fritz Peterson with a record of 3-13. Add this to the mix: no Mickey Mantle in the New York lineup, and a bunch of deflated Yankees playing out the string in a long season up against a jubilant White Sox squad in the heat of a pennant race who just won a thriller. Looks grim for the Bronx Bombers (cool nickname, one must give the devil his due).

But it looked even grimmer for the Sox nine innings later: New York 2, Chicago 1. Thus you'd have the scores of the double-headers neatly presented in the next day's paper in this fashion: Chicago, 3-1; New York, 2-2. I'm compelled to display this for several reasons; first, the enthusiasm and suspense a double-header score presents as I quickly try to decipher sweep or split (it does take an enjoyable second or two to figure this out); secondly, to prove that double-headers did exist at one time; and thirdly, to prepare readers what this format means should they ever come across them. I find it somewhat amusing at times that it seems that the only double-header scores are now associated with high schools who endure wind chills of 30 degrees to get in both games.

The Yankee victory came courtesy of Peterson's two-hitter, both collected by Tommie Agee. Tom Tresh (as kids we cleverly referred to him as Tom Trash) trashed the White Sox by scoring the winning run in the eighth after tripling. So Fritz Peterson, from De Kalb, IL, whose claim to fame was swapping wives with another ballplayer, sent us home mildly disappointed.

All was not bad, however, even in a loss. For starters, I got to stay up way past my bed time. More significantly, this second game marked the first time I ever sat in the upper deck. My dad escorted me there at the conclusion of game 2. He probably figured that it's now safe to take a little kid up there; since it was a weeknight and getting late, the fights would be at a minimum. I remember only seeing one or two that night, no kidding. (but keep in mind we're up there for only a couple of innings).

Little did I know that this view would change me for life. Just like you can characterize people by the responses given to a dichotomy: boxers or briefs, Leno or Letterman, Beatles or Stones, Ginger or Mary Ann; a person's preference of lower vs. upper deck can speak volumes. Sitting upstairs approached the thrill of my very first game, that's how much fun it was. The perspective overwhelmed me. Seeing the entire field at once and in front of you allowed you to note the positioning of the defenders, the immensity of the outfield, and even the crispness of a fastball. From now on, I'm an upper-deck boy.

GAME 17: August 26, 1967

Little League. What's the first thing to come to mind when you hear those two words? Think of the movies done on this concept; think of the jokes said about it; think of the hysteria associated with it; and perhaps most of all, think of the politics. A kid I was working with one summer captured it well with this simple and innocent statement, "Hey, Mr. O'Donnell, I made the All-Star team in my town, and *my dad's not even a coach.*"

Now the purpose of this literary endeavor is to reminisce about the Big Leagues, not the Little Leagues. Nevertheless, the two have been known to overlap, as they did for me on a hot summer's day in late August of '67. The Chicago American League Ballclub was sponsoring "Little League Day" at Comiskey Park. Interesting concept. Transporting busloads of kids decked out in their Little League uniform, which generally consisted of a T-shirt with a professional team's name on front, and the sponsor's name on back. Throw in a baseball cap with the letter of the town highlighted and a pair of gym shoes, and you were in business. Fun for kids, migraines for adults. (illustration to follow).

A confession is in order (remember this day did fall on a Saturday, so Confessions are fitting). The admission I must make is this: the outcome of the game was a distant second that day to have as much fun as possible with my friends. I didn't get cheated. In fact, since pure joy was the order of the day, I almost did not keep score.

One thing that stands out about these outings is seat location. Of all truisms I've come across, this is one of the truest and one of my favorites: "You get what you pay for." Well, since we Little Leaguers didn't pay anything (maybe my folks did, but I thought this might have been a freebie), binoculars came in handy. After a forty minute walk from the main concourse to our seats, with a strong set of binoculars you might be able to make out the dirt part of the infield. What bothers me a little is this: plenty of other seats were available as the crowd was announced at 12-13 thousand. So if management wasn't going to invite us down to the good seats, we'd just go ahead and invite ourselves, wreaking havoc on the ushers.

But once the game was underway we tried to be good Little Leaguers and watch the game without incident. Situated in these seats kilometers from home plate, a situation arose which I nor my ball playing brethren would soon forget. Somewhere in the middle of the game, Mike Ryan of the Red Sox was trying to build on an already commanding lead. This catcher of the Bosox got way in front of a pitch and drove it with authority. Remember that the batter now is as close to us as Neptune, so when the ball starts traveling in our direction, we're overcome with awe and wonder. At first, the sphere is a pill, then a golf ball, and ultimately a baseball as our eyes became as wide as beach balls. This marks a memorable first: a big leaguer hitting a ball heading directly toward me. Isn't it interesting how you hope and dream of catching a foul ball some day, and when that opportunity finally presents itself, your dreams give way to survival. You want the reward and prize and esteem of snaring a baseball, of course, but you don't want to break multiple bones in the process. If a ball is traveling to the extremities of mammoth Comiskey Park, you didn't have to be an Einstein or a master of word problems to realize that the ball must have some "giddy-up" behind it. My dilemma was quickly resolved: I chose survival by ducking out of the way and hoping to grab the trophy on the ricochet (which, by the way, is a common phenomenon). I thought it might bounce off two or three hands, heads, and heinies, and then I'd snatch the ball as it was barely rolling.

No such luck. The kid sitting directly in from of me ended up with the ball. Galahad and the Holy Grail had nothing on him and his foul ball. If you wanted to see envy personified, come to the section at that moment in time and look at our faces. Heck, I need not project, look at my face now. If you gave the average Little Leaguer the choice between a bank account or catching a foul ball at a major league game, what do you think the answer would be? A few <u>might</u> ask how much is in the bank, but the majority would take the ball in a heartbeat.

Now I grew up with a logical friend named George who was a very good hitter himself, and he used to wonder why people would go bonkers in the stands for a ball that they could buy in a store for a few bucks. Being one of those people he was describing, I never had a good answer for him. He made sense. But then I had this other friend who would race inside the ballpark once the gates opened, locate a strategic spot close to the outfield foul lines, and wait for long fouls during batting practice. He brought his mitt to the game well into his high school years, and felt no shame. Funny, but I never had to justify irrational foul ball behavior to him.

Back to this kid who was now the owner of a real major league baseball. An array of feelings engulfed us. Relief, at having survived. Excitement, at being so close to fame. Wonder, as if "I wonder if we got on television." And jealousy, gladly trading my left arm for that ball, maybe even my Billy Williams' baseball card for it.

Sharks to blood could not be quicker than other kids to that ball. Droves of little leaguers, from several sections away, swarmed to the scene. They came to see, touch, and smell the ball. If adults weren't around, they probably would sneak a taste, too. Next were the proposals. "If you give me that ball, I'll give you this mitt." "I'll let you have my Cracker Jack and the prize inside if I can hold the ball for an inning." One kid I knew played Dr. Ben Casey, "You better have that arm looked at. Here, I'll just hold the ball for you while you go get some help." But this kid wasn't born yesterday. I was watching him closely and he wasn't falling for any of this. People who wind up with foul balls are nobody's fool. This lucky kid was neither too gullible nor too possessive about his prized possession. His arm did smart a little, but it's a small price to pay for such a reward. I doubt if owners of both ball clubs combined could offer fair compensation for that ball, simply because it was his when it could have belonged to the other 12,390 people in attendance.

Unfortunately, that ball was the highlight of the game. The Sox lost to the Sox. (In my adult years, I was greatly distressed that the Boston ball club was also referred to as the Sox. How dare them! It's kind of like a pretty girl calling out your name only to find out that some other guy has the same name as you. The nerve).

I saw history that day, however. Remember a few games back when the discussion centered on Red Sox futility? Well, here's proof for that charge: Boston's victory on this day pushed them into first place for the first time since 1949. That's eighteen years of looking up at someone in the standings. What makes it even more baffling was the caliber of some Bosox players: in left field alone, you had either a T. Williams or a C. Yastrzemski, pick your legend. Also, you figure that in one of those 18 seasons the franchise would sneak to 1st by winning the first 3 or 4 games in April. But I suppose all that frustration made '67 all the sweeter.

The well-known pennant race of 1967 was in full bloom on our "Little League Day." The White Sox contended on pitching and defense. In this 5-game showdown with Boston, Gary Peters got KO'ed in game 1 on Friday, not making it out of the 2nd inning. Yet, the paper reports he'd be returning on Sunday to pitch one of the games in the twin-bill. Pitching on one day's rest is not something you see too much anymore. Nor will you see the same pitcher face the same team twice in the same series, unless it's post-season. But we're talking the scrappy White Sox here, managed by Eddie Stanky.

This game marked the second time in a week that I watched Joe Horlen go down to defeat. First, Fritz Peterson of the Yankees, and now, Jerry Stephenson. The difference, however, was clear. The 2-1 setback was a tough luck loss, conjuring up a slew of "what-if's" and "if-only's." This 6-2 was not as close as the score might suggest. I recall the Red Sox spending much of the afternoon playing ring around the bases. This happens when the starter surrenders 10 hits in less than 5 innings. Over the years baseball people accept this as one of those games that you're just not going to win. If there was a stat in baseball that showed time of possession, the Red Sox would have clearly dominated. Not that painful if you can be philosophical and resign yourself to it, and in Chicago, we've had plenty of practice. Besides, being surrounded by friends and teammates and experiencing a long foul ball as a close encounter made for a special day.

GAME 18: August 29, 1967

Sure enough, after a flurry of Sox games (three in one week) my mom decided it was time for an outing to Wrigley Field. I detected one other pattern about our baseball trips: as summer approached fall, trips to the ballpark increased. Going to the ballgame seemed to be a way of denying the inevitable schedules of school and serious business. Let's extend the summer as much as possible; let's get to a game while there's still time.

As a parental unit myself, I found cramming things in the last couple of weeks in summer to be the norm. Even though George Harrison wasn't a Chicagoan, he had me in mind when he sings that, " ... it's been a long, cold, lonely winter." And what better way to postpone winter by cheering your lungs out at a ballgame?

Sadly, cheering for the home team was becoming less and less frequent with losses piling up. This next game was your typical painful, let's-wait-til-the-end-to-blow-it Cub defeat. A headline in the **Chicago Tribune** reads, "Astros score 5 in 8th for 5-3 triumph." How often in your lifetime have the Cubs failed to hold a lead in the late innings? I have a wager for you: it begins with both sides having a dollar. Now I'll give you a dime for every game the Cubs won that they should have lost; and in return you give me a nickel for every time that the Cubs lose a game that they should have won. I think we'd agree on who would go broke first.

Speaking of blowing leads, the pressure of the closer is unreal. Maybe that's why, outside of a Mariano Rivera, Rollie Fingers, Trevor Hoffmann, etc, closers have the life expectancy of a gnat at the major league level. Imagine a position where all the fans and teammates are counting on you, and if you do well, it's basically taken for granted. But in the event of failure, you single-handedly have ruined the past three hours for thousands of people. Who would want that job?

That being said, it still is frustrating beyond description how one team can hold another team scoreless for seven innings, then proceed to get ripped when down to the final outs. It's even more baffling and frustrating how often that team happens to be the Cubs. Blowing leads late in the game is not a daily occurrence for this team, but neither has it been rare.

Houston, for an expansion team, had some "mahty fahn" players. Joe Morgan starred in the early stages of his hall-of-fame career. Doug Rader, a **Ball Four** character, performed well at third base. (He's also credited with the phrase, "Winning Ugly", to describe the play of the 1983 White Sox). A young Larry Dierker showed a lot promise. But two stars stood out: Rusty Staub and the "Toy Cannon", Jimmy Wynn. Wynn, about the size of a Willie McCovey leg or a Frank Howard bicep, pounded homers with regularity. A truly remarkable feat, this was, and not just because of his stature. The Astrodome, where Wynn played half his games was the National League's answer to Comiskey Park with its Grand Canyon-like dimensions. And since play was always indoors (a phenomena that must have driven mothers crazy: "no ball playing inside"), there was no wind to assist Wynn.

Jimmy was why the Astros Wynn this game. He homered with two men on base and two men out in the eighth. The pitcher victimized was the one guy on the Cubs that Wynn could post up, Chuck "Twiggy" Hartenstein. This late inning misfortune ruined a solid pitching performance by a guy I appreciated for many years, Joe Niekro. I remember looking at the back of Niekro's baseball card one year and thinking football scores. (My sixth grade nun looked at the front of his card and declared him "cute." I wonder if I could have traded him for a St. Francis holy card, since I did have doubles of Niekro. Cards were brought to school to make transactions prior to the lunch period trading deadline). Niekro's first two win-loss records were Bear-like numbers: 10-7 in '67 and 14-10 in '68. Consider his upside:

- Young
- Effective
- Playing for a franchise where quality pitching was scarce
- Related to Phil, so maybe genetically gifted

- Cute, according to a nun

When you take into account all these factors, you might come to the conclusion that he'd be with the Cubs for many years. If so, you thought wrong. Niekro was traded for Dick Selma, who didn't pitch very long but was an enthusiastic cheerleader for the Bleacher Bums. The sad career totals look like this: Selma: 42 wins, Niekro: 221 wins. Now who would you rather have? In fairness, Niekro bounced around for a few years with a few teams before prospering with the Astros. And that success hinged on his learning and perfecting the knuckle ball. Still, couldn't the baseball people in the Cub organization recognize his potential? I mean, 200 or so wins over the next decade and a half could have come in handy. Besides, not once did I ever hear any religious refer to Selma as cute.

No doubt that baseball thrives on trivia. Insignificant or inconsequential are not part of the vocabulary of a die-hard baseball fan. When I went to a game in these early years, I almost always noticed at least one thing that intrigued or enchanted me. This day it had nothing to do with the outcome—a Cub loss in the late innings is not exactly fodder for Ripley. No, what struck me this day is what struck a baserunner. Rusty Staub, a baserunner at first, was struck with a batted ball. At this point in my life, I had never seen nor heard of that happening, not in the alley, not in the playground, not on TV, and absolutely not in person. Later, Shawon Dunston of the Cubs seemed to have this down to a science, but back then it was unimaginable. This mishap transpired at a critical point in the contest. The game was on the line and the batter cracked what looked like a ground single between Banks and Beckert. But hold on, the ball suddenly changed directions. It took a sharp left and was headed toward second base. Staub's body language reflected dejection and embarrassment. My scorecard and I are struck dumb. I needed Jack Brickhouse to explain what I just saw and how to score it. At times like these professional sports should consider taking a page out of kids' rules by instituting a "Do over."

Professional baseball eschews the "do over" policy but does something weirder. The defense gets an out, though it hardly earned it. And even more bizarre, the batter is credited with a single. That made no sense to me then, and very little forty years later. Can't you see the day when a pitcher takes a no-hitter into the ninth inning and issues a two-out walk. Now since the team on the field is leading 4-0, the right side of the infield is playing behind the runner. Then, **CRACK**, a solid two-hopper headed in the general direction of the second basemen, but **SMACK,** the runner on first is nailed in the left buttock as he races for second. (Of course, this is all done as accidentally as a high stick comes up and smacks the opposing hockey player who has just scored his fourth goal of the game). What transpires then is the gloomiest celebration of a victory in the annals of the game. A game won but a no-hitter lost. I could envision the runner being both congratulated and chastised for his rear accomplishment. Stranger things have happened, I think.

Following this defeat, two vivid events developed outside the ballpark. First, I got lost, seriously lost. The kind of lost when panic sets in and you doubt if you'll ever see your family again. I was crying my eyes out, and this time it had nothing to do with a Chicago defeat. So upset was I that people started to look at me, point, and have concerned looks on their faces. If you're from a big city, you know it must be serious for strangers to show this kind of concern. No one talked to me; but registered that "I-hope-this-kid-finds-his-family-cuz-I-don't-want-to-get-involved" look. Their non-involvement didn't bother me, though, what I really wanted was my mom. After what seemed to be a ten hour separation, which was closer to two minutes in reality time, my mom found me. Relief ran through me while embarrassment ran through her. I caused quite a scene.

The other event that I remember was getting autographs from the *visiting* team. I never considered getting enemy signatures before, but there we were outside the visitors clubhouse after my wandering adventure. (Maybe my mom was too humiliated for us to stick around the Cubs' side of the ballpark). So why not try to get some Astros to sign my ball. Were they not major leaguers? I considered it unusual but not a defilement.

I secured two signatures on the sweet-smelling sphere, with the more famous one belonging to Norm Miller. He started that day, played left field, threw a guy out at home, and went 0-4. For the season, Norm hit .205, so an 0-4 day would not cause tremendous distress. Miller ended up with a .238 lifetime batting average with very little run production. Surprisingly, he lasted ten seasons; he must have been a defensive wizard. Or perhaps it was for comic relief, since he too is mentioned several times in Jim Bouton's **Ball Four**. Whatever the case, he did help a young boy overcome the pain of a Cub loss and serious separation anxiety with a neatly written signature on my ball.

The less famous autograph obtained that day belonged to Bruce Von Hoff, a pitcher. I'm proud to say that Bruce has only one more major league hit than me (1), and we're tied for wins with zero. His next major league save, and I don't think he'll have many more chances, will be his first. Von Hoff appeared in 13 games, pitched 53 innings, and finished with an 0-3 record with a 5.06 ERA. Still, wouldn't you trade a lot of your past with his? He can say that he played major league baseball.

As a nine-year old, that put him somewhere between God and the president. He was a major leaguer, and more importantly, a major leaguer who signed my ball. Von Hoff and Miller may not be in the class of Staub, Wynn, or Morgan (Mike Cuellar was also on this team), but they were nice enough to make a distraught nine-year old feel a little better.

As my spectating season comes to a close, a couple of streaks are made manifest. The streaky success of my first dozen or so games has already been documented. But toward the end of '67, the honeymoon comes to an abrupt halt. An occasional win sprinkled amidst a blizzard of defeats becomes the norm for the next few decades. "Weeelll," as Samantha Stevens in **Bewitched** used to say, it was fun while it lasted.

The other streak that's been fairly consistent is simply the attendance pattern at games. I doubt if it's that unusual, but I noticed that I'll go months without seeing a game, then experience of flurry of games in a couple of weeks. I suppose my folks had to get their fix of baseball while they could. The summer of '67 proves this theory: not one game did I see until August. Then, WHAM, a furious charge of baseball trips just as my school sentence was about to resume. Toward the end of '67, watching five games in a span of a couple of weeks was fun; seeing the losses start to pile up wasn't.

POST-SEASON, 1967

One thing I like doing as a teacher is to play word association. Here's one for you: what's the first thing that pops into your mind when you hear this: 1967? Now if you specialize in American history, you might say Vietnam, LBJ, or Civil Rights. Broadway folks might think HAIR or "Aquarius" (it took me four tries and a dictionary to spell it correctly). Mrs. Robinson and the whereabouts of Joe DiMaggio come to mind for movie-goers. But 1967 is a no-brainer for this baseball fan: the American League pennant race. It's like this: 1967—AL Pennant Race, AL Pennant Race—1967. They're inseparable. They're woven together in the tapestry of time. I can't say with any authority that this was the best conclusion to a baseball season, but I do know that I've never witnessed a closer race with more teams.

The memory persists because four teams had a very legitimate chance to win the pennant going into the last week of the season. Remember, no consolation places were available — no multi-divisional leaders or wild-card positions. It was first place or forget it. In fact, I remember some old-timers telling me the World Series was often anti-climatic—the pennant was the thing. And this logic makes sense; why get worked up over one opponent in the span of seven games when you just grabbed first from nine opponents over 162 games?

One of these four teams was our very own White Sox. Now we acknowledge that baseball is all about pitching; however, if it was just pitching alone, the Sox (White) would have won hands down. Ponder this: the worst ERA among the Sox top three starters was 2.47! And a 2.47 would get you a record of 10-13 (see Tommy John for details). Gary Peters was 16-11 with a 2.28 ERA, and Joe Horlen finished 19-7 with a 2.06 ERA. Not only were they ranked 1-2-3 on the team, they were 1-2-4 in the entire league! (Some of you are guessing, I know, who took the bronze. Here's a clue: he pitched for Cleveland. I bet you're still having trouble. The answer: Sonny Siebert). For a little icing on Horlen's ERA cake, he tossed a no-hitter against a very potent Tiger lineup in early September. (I recall getting the news from the back porch as I played in the alley behind my grandma's house).

When you look at the numbers of the big three pitchers, simple arithmetic holds that if Chicago were to score just three runs per game, they'd win at least ¾ of their games. (The other pitchers in the four-man rotation yielded over three runs per game). But it's not that simple. Asking the Sox offense to generate three runs per game is akin to asking Twiggy (the real one, not Hartenstein) to eat three square meals per day. She may do it, but it won't be every day, and she definitely won't go beyond that. Seldom were the blow-outs that summer.

Aside from the White Sox, the other contenders included two teams that I liked mucho—the Tigers and the Twins—and one team no me gusto mucho—the Red Sox. These three clubs were balanced. Bona fide sluggers found in each lineup: Killebrew, Oliva, and Allison; Kaline, Horton, and Cash; Yaz, Tony C., and Scott. It makes you wonder how in the world the Sox could compete. Chicago's leading hitters tore up the league at a .241 clip—Don Buford and Ken Berry. Translation: the club was fortunate if their *best* hitters went 1 for 4. This illustrates just how dominant the Sox pitching had to be, how capable their defense must have been, and how this feisty Stanky team did compete. The question was this: could one David beat out three Goliaths over a 162 game schedule?

No, not this year. The White Sox were the first to go. Adding to this sting was this: the executors of the Sox demise were two doormats of the league. The official elimination came on Friday night home game vs. the Washington Senators (the Washington Redskins, I think, won more games that year than the Senators). The mortal blow, however, came at the hand of Charlie Finley's Kansas City Athletics. Two low-scoring defeats (what else?) in a twi-night doubleheader all but finished off the Sox.

That left the Tigers vs. the Angels in Michigan, and the marquee match-up of Minnesota at Boston during the final weekend. One of the more vivid memories I have is watching the Twins-Red Sox do battle on NBC's "Game of the Week." (for the umpteenth time in my childhood I got to hear comments about the Green Monster in a nationally televised game). I sat glued to the TV set in a buddy's basement. My friend's name was Norm, and I truly enjoyed watching the game with him and his dad. We were all pulling hard for the Twins. I don't remember why, but a significant part of our conversation centered on Ron Santo's pizza. In those days Santo peddled pizza at the grocery store and the ballpark. Although it looked and smelled great, I always opted for the "red hots" at Wrigley Field (I doubt Ron's pizza would sell at Sox Park). Now Norm and his dad happened to be big Ron Santo fans, and even bigger fans of his pizza. In fact the dad boldly predicted something in the early stages of this contest that I won't soon forget. He said that "Killer" on the Twins was about to jack one because he just ate one of Santo's pizzas. Noticing Killebrew's girth, neither statement seemed beyond belief. CRACK—sure enough, Killebrew launched a pitch over the Green Monster to put the Twins ahead of Boston in the game and the pennant race. Incidentally, Killer also put himself one ahead of Yaz in the tight home run race. After the cheering subsided, I started looking at my friend's dad as some sort of pizza and home run Nostradamus.

On this Saturday afternoon, the Twins sailed along and it looked like the game and the pennant would be theirs. Then disaster struck. Minnesota starter Jim Kaat, in total control of the Boston hitters, had to leave the game due to an injury. I'm convinced, to this day, that if "Kitty" Kaat did not get hurt, the Twins play the Cardinals in the '67 World Series. But, alas, everything that could go wrong at the point did. I guess there's no one in the AL that was going to block Boston's "Impossible Dream" season. The Red Sox scored enough runs against Minnesota's bullpen to steal the game. Then on Sunday, Yaz and Lonborg finished off my heroes from the Land of Lakes. The other team I liked, the Tigers, were extinguished by the Angels. So that meant that the Bosox were headed to the World Series. To quote some famous author somewhere, "Yuck."

This unfortunate series of events meant that for the first time since '64, I'd be rooting for a National League team. By coincidence, both appearances were by the Cardinals. I've come to favor the AL over the years, I believe, for this twisted reason: I've seen too many NL teams over the years beat up on the Cubs. How could I root for anybody that's got Cub blood on their hands? The Sox, on the other hand, seem to hold their own against AL opponents.

If anyone out there starts up a fantasy World Series baseball team, here's what you do: draft Bob Gibson. Then draft Lou Brock. Then get seven other players to fill the other slots. (a George Brett or a Roberto Clemente would be nice additions). But it really doesn't matter; give me Gibson and Brock and seven stiffs and I'll take my chances. No lie. Growing up it seemed as if these two, by themselves, teamed up to beat New York, Boston, and almost Detroit. It's kind of like that scene in **Shane** when it's just Shane and the kid's dad, but they beat up all the bad guys. Put Gibby and Brock in the middle of the room, and that's who I put my money on.

Having said that, give Boston a ton of credit. They battled St. Louis to the limit on the strength of Yaz's hitting and Lonborg's pitching. It came down to a Game 7, but in that one game, Gibson takes over by hitting a homer and pitching a three-hitter to lead the Cards to a 7-2 victory and another world championship.

For the record, Yaz concluded the regular season by hitting over .500 during the final two weeks of the season. He then cooled off in the Series, hitting only .400 over seven games. Thus his Triple Crown season concluded in fitting fashion (in truth, Killebrew did tie Yaz in homers). Lonborg delivered in the Series as well, with a 2-1 mark and a 2.63 ERA. But they met their match with Brock and Gibson. Brock hit .414 and scored eight times in the seven games. Gibson's ERA? 1.00, to go along with his Game 7 heroics. I've always enjoyed the playoffs in sports, and especially the World Series, because the great ballplayers play their best in the biggest games. Let's say that if my life depended on one game, I'd want Gibson pitching that game. I would just wait until after the game to tell him that I'm a Chicago fan.

PRESEASON, 1968

If 1967 was the year of the pennant race, then 1968 had to be the Year of the Pitcher. Plenty of praise has already been heaped upon Bob Gibson, but his accomplishment this year is incomprehensible: over 300 innings pitched with an ERA of 1.12. Sometimes we baseball freaks overdo the stat thing, but I ask you to contemplate these two numbers again—it amounts to barely over a run per nine innings for 33 complete games pitched. Incredible.

But even this took a back seat to the pitcher/organist/ Pepsi-drinker known as Denny McLain. Arguments surface frequently regarding baseball's unbreakable records. Two numbers jump out often: 56 and 191. They represent Joe DiMaggio's hitting streak and Hack Wilson's RBI's for one season. (Incidentally, the year of the hitting streak reveals a fact you might find in Ripley's: did you know that Ted Williams hit for a higher average than DiMaggio over those 56 games? The year of the hitting streak was also the last year of a .400 hitter). With the untouchables of 56 and 191, I think you can safely say that Denny McLain is the last 30-game winner that baseball will see in a long, long time. Just look how hard it is to win 20. Why, some *franchises* as of 2008 have yet to boast a 20-game winner. The math suggests that with five-man rotations, more relief pitching with fewer complete games, there just aren't going to be enough opportunities for a 30-win season. Fewer decisions and more no-decisions have been the trend for some time now, so Denny McLain's accomplishment in the year of the pitcher looks pretty safe.

GAME 19: June 13, 1968

Since tickets were not bought in advance, going to games was not always a sure thing. Some days we definitely were going; other days we might be going; infrequently it was a spontaneous affair; and then there were those days like this day. First we were going, and then we weren't. A setback, but it meant more time to play baseball on a tiny field called Murph's in the 'hood. Round about the third inning, here comes my old man in his business suit strolling toward the batter's box. Now talk about oddities. Here was my dad on a field where the oldest person who ever set foot was thirteen. It was the middle of a work day, and he was all decked out, and he was requesting the honor of my presence (or something like that) on an excursion to Wrigley Field. The only time I ever saw my dad at home on a Thursday morning was Thanksgiving. I swear that I've had dreams where I'm in my underwear that made more sense than this scene.

But, next thing you know, we're at our customary spot along the third base grandstands watching Frank Reberger of the Cubs preparing to mow down the

Cincinnati Reds. Frank Reberger, today's starting pitcher, THE Frank Reberger. Some days you get Fergie Jenkins or Gary Peters, other days you get Frank Reberger. I was banking on the Reds' pitching being worse than the Cubs.

It was. Ernie and Santo knocked the ball around the park. Santo homered and scored three times; Ernie went 3 for 3 with a homer and 4 RBI's. The other tater in the game belonged to a young rookie catcher on the Reds named Johnny Bench. Ever hear of him? I remember my dad praising Bench, and earnest compliments from him was about as common as snow in April. It has been known to happen. Actually, my dad commented favorably on two rookies breaking in when I was a youth: Bench and George Brett. I'd say he's 2 for 2.

A few years before the Reds earned the label as the "Big Red Machine," I feared them more than any other opponent. I couldn't comprehend why a lineup that featured Rose, Alex Johnson, Tony Perez, Lee May, Vada Pinson, Tommie Helms, and Bench did not make the World Series an annual ritual.

Now, upon further review, I know why. Tony Cloninger, starting pitcher, yielded 5 hits, 2 walks, 2 wild pitches, and a hit batter in three innings of work. Later, in the 7th inning, the Reds committed as many errors as the Cubs made outs, which led to three unearned runs. Defense and pitching, pitching and defense. As Cub fans know all too well, but probably hate to admit, if you lack pitching and defense you will lack championships.

Speaking of pitching, it's obvious that Leo Durocher did not have absolute confidence in Mr. Reberger. Here's a young pitcher given a 5-1 cushion after three innings, but was yanked in the 4th. True, he was rocked for 7 hits and 3 runs, and you can't argue with a Cub win. But permit me to second guess a deceased manager in a meaningless game played many years ago. If a young pitcher isn't allowed to work out of jams with the kind of non-pitching and non-defense the Reds showed that day—how will he learn? A common rap against Leo is that he favored veterans and eschewed youth, making it difficult for younger players to develop on the Cubs. I doubt he would have given Fergie such a quick hook. I just remember a Phil Regan or Ted Abernathy bailing out a young Reberger, Rich Nye, or Joe Niekro while the older starters like Hands, Holtzman, and Jenkins were given the chance to pitch out of jams.

But all's well that ends well, according to Jack Brickhouse, and today's win improved my record against a good Cincinnati team to 3-0. It would reach 4-0 a few years later when Billy Williams slugged a walk-off homer in the bottom of the 10th. I still remember Bobby Tolan's sad expression as he watched the ball sail into the catwalk. I watched that game with a good friend named Pete who was a huge Bobby Tolan fan (don't ask me why) and he shouted consoling words to the Red outfielder as he trotted off the field.

Little did I know that wins from this point on against Cincinnati would be few and far between. The Cubs struggle against most teams, but over the years my record against three clubs—the Reds, Dodgers, and Phillies—is something like 10–32. Another ouch.

This summer sizzled with material for history textbooks. Two assassinations, the confrontational Democratic convention in Chicago, and 2001 Space Odyssey which impressed a buddy's brother and disappointed my folks. Again, I was too young for all this. Call it the innocence and sheltering of youth. I'd throw my mitt on my Stingray and pedal off to play more ball.

Some say baseball imitates life; 1968 proves it. Bizarre events in the world parallel strange things in the baseball world:

1. Catfish Hunter tosses the first perfect game in the American League since 1922.

2. The Cubs and Sox did a flip-flop in the standings: the Cubs are now decent and the Sox aren't.

3. My dad goes to Wrigley Field when the Sox aren't playing; and my mom attends *two* games on the South Side.

Full moons in full bloom?

GAMES 20 & 21 July 24, 1968

Extenuating circumstances explains my mother's unorthodox behavior of attending not one but two Sox games. First, it was a twi-nite doubleheader, so it only meant one trip to Comiskey. Secondly, she heard on the radio as the first game was under way that between games the Sox brass was giving away free birthday cake to the fans in honor of Hoyt Wilhelm's recent birthday (he turned 45 a couple days earlier). Now my mom takes to dessert as my dad takes to beer. Not too many things are higher on her list than baked goods. So to endure a White Sox doubleheader in return for some free cake made the evening a lot easier to swallow. This is how I recall broadcasters marketing doubleheaders in the early innings of game one: "Plenty of baseball still to be played tonight. So if you're in the area, why don't you come by to catch most of game one and all of game 2." Hillside wasn't exactly in the area, but the bakeries were closed for the evening, so off we go.

Time for some stereotypes: the most recent Cub game epitomized contests at Wrigley Field: 12 runs, 3 homers in 9 innings. Clearly the offense dominates. Now for a vintage Sox doubleheader: 2 games, 18 innings, and 2 teams combine for 4 runs. Only the White Sox in the mid to late 60's could hold a team to three runs over two games and lose twice. These were the real hitless wonders.

On Hoyt's big day, the offense played like citizens twice his age. Now to give Oakland their props, they were in the process of developing a very fine team; some have even called it a dynasty. Even if the opponent wasn't quite "Murderer's Row" on offense, the pitching from that night was a sign of things to come. If you thought that Catfish pitched that night, it'd be a good guess, but wrong. Vida Blue would come along later ('71) and Kenny Holtzman still belonged to the Cubs (oddly enough, the guy Holtzman was traded for, Rick Monday, played for Oakland that night and drove in the only run in the first game. The **Chicago Tribune** indicated that at this time, Monday was the only hitter in the league hitting .300 or better. Remember, the year of the pitcher).

The A's hurlers who stymied the Sox that night were Jim "Cotton" Nash and John "Blue Moon" Odom. Their pitching was good; their nicknames were better. Nash threw a complete game, four hit shutout in the opener, with all hits being singles. In the nightcap an RBI single by Luis Aparicio in the 8th drove home Sandy Alomar Senior, father of Sandy Alomar Junior. This spoiled Odom's whitewash and tied the score. It also broke a streak of 37 scoreless innings by the Sox, which is the equivalent of four straight shutouts. So while the A's pitching deserves some credit, the Sox had this knack of making pitchers with names like "Cotton" and "Blue Moon" look like "Big Train" and "Rapid Robert."

The Athletics picked an opportune time to evolve into prominence. Their nicknames (don't forget "Campy"), their mustaches (Rollie Fingers), their clubhouse unrest, and their rebel ways epitomized that genre in history.

And of course the uniforms. This was a team made for colored television. I remember how their gold, green, and Sunday white uniforms were condemned by purists as softball outfits. They never bothered me. Granted that they were no match for the striking Cardinal red, the "Swinging A's" style did provide a colorful contrast to the dirty gray clothes donned by visiting ball clubs.

I was never much into style or fashion (just ask my wife) but the A's appearance caught even my attention at an early 70's All-Star game. Prior to the game, the ritual includes the introduction of players and subsequent jogs to one of the base lines. The sight of seeing the A's all-stars—Campaneris, Hunter, Reggie Jackson, etc.—emerge from the dugout in different colored jerseys was just plain cool.

Charlie Finley got plenty of publicity in his day and most of it negative. I doubt if I would like to play for him, based on ample criticism directed his way from his players. But I do think he deserves credit for his innovation and attempting new things that brought color and life into the game. (I recall one that didn't make the cut: colored baseballs so they could stand out more in the green grass). And, the success of his teams surely could not be overlooked. He three-peated long before there was the word, three-peat.

A recap of the evening's highlights (this won't take long), through the eyes of Hoyt Wilhelm:

- Hoyt sets a record for the most appearances in a game as a pitcher
- Hoyt receives a lot of presents between games, including a gigantic birthday cake and salami (calling to mind those witty *Alka-Seltzer* commercials)

- Between games Hoyt gets his picture taken with his family, which includes my Little League nemesis, Jimmy.

- Hoyt gives up the winning run in the ninth inning, but at least this time it's not on a passed ball.

A pretty eventful night for Hoyt; a lackluster evening for his teammates. And even though the Sox lost twice, the cake tasted pretty good—yellow cake with white frosting, I recall. As a baseball fan growing up in Chicago, you learn to take whatever victories you can get.

GAME 22: August 1, 1968

How times do change. The **Chicago Tribune** reports that an eight-game home stand on the North side averaged 22,000 fans per contest. This is labeled a financial success. Three to four decades later, if the Cubs were to draw 22,000 fans, who knows how Cub ownership would respond? I just know it wouldn't be a financial success.

An old adage in baseball says that you're going to win 60 games and lose 60 games, no matter what. The key is what a team does in those other 42 games; that separates contenders from pretenders. Today was one of those days that had victory all written all over it. Timely hitting, effective pitching, and solid defense resulted in my favorite score: 4-1, Cubs over Houston.

The stars of this game included Ron Santo, with 2 RBI singles; Randy Hundley, who played long ball (homered in the second) and small ball (2 sacrifice bunts); Don Kessinger, who singled twice, scored twice, and tripled once; and the combined pitching of Joe Niekro (7 IP, 1 ER, and 11th win) and Phil Regan (2 IP, Save #15). It wasn't a flawless performance–one walk, one error, seven hits by the other team—but it was the type of game that a manager almost doesn't like because there's not a whole lot to scold the team in order to keep them sharp.

(Being a fan, that confused me; being a coach that made sense). Just a snappy win (2 hours and 16 minutes), the kind that good teams pull off with regularity. Were the Cubs becoming a good team?

A minor footnote to this game examines one of the hitting stars for the Cubs, Ron Santo. In this game we see Santo snap out of a slump against an unlikely opponent with some unlikely instruction. The advice for Santo's hitting came from his manager, Leo Durocher, who Babe Ruth referred to as the "All-American out." Now hitting instructors need not be batting champions, but the scenario of Durocher helping Santo with his hitting strikes me as odd. The difference in eras, age, power, style, ability, etc. suggests a huge disconnect; but just a minor tip, as it seems in this case, can produce big results. Or was it a coincidence? No matter, because if Durocher points out something, and Santo makes the adjustment and enjoys success, Durocher's credibility in the eyes of his player escalates.

The other surprising circumstance has to do with Santo's success coming against Dave Giusti, the Astro starting pitcher. I've collected perhaps thousands of mental images of Cubs/Sox players succeeding or failing in all sorts of situations. One lasting image I have is Santo facing Dave Giusti, but this time he's a reliever for the Pittsburgh Pirates. He's on the team nicknamed the "Lumber Company" for their prowess on offense that allowed their pitching and defense a lot of room for error, which they sometimes needed. Anyway, I can see Giusti in his square Pirate cap of gold and black, bearing down to face Santo with the tying run on second base and the winning run on first. Giusti throws his palm ball, Santo hits it sharply at the shortstop who feeds the second baseman (likely Rennie Stennet or Dave Cash) who relays his throw to the first baseman (take your pick: Oliver,

Stargell, Robertson) and the ball game is over. I swear that scene is etched in my brain. Not a heart-breaker, just a disappointment that if so deeply embedded, I must have seen it more than once. However, on this day, Santo bested Giusti, and selfishly, I was there to share in Ronnie's success.

GAME 23: August 10, 1968

This next Sox game tops the list for "best stuff happening on the way home." It was the annual Little League Day at the ballpark. Our contingent from Hillside had busloads of kids returning on a hot Saturday afternoon in August. I really don't think that the game itself (a White Sox loss) had anything to do with what was to follow.

My seat on the bus was prime—the very last seat, passenger side. From this vantage point I got a great view of all the action. The adult chaperones congregated near the front of the bus, probably a bit weary of Little League ballplayers at this point of the trip. This critical maneuver left virtually free reign to a bunch of 6th and 7th grade boys at the back bus. Big mistake.

It began innocently enough. Remember those bus windows that require both hands and a few cuss words to operate? And inevitably, the window is pushed down too far or not far enough, requiring more pairs of hands and more cuss words. Well, after what seemed like an hour I finally arrived at the ideal window position. I needed some reward after this effort, so for entertainment value, I took the cap of one of my neighborhood pals (Dan was his name) and flung it out the window. I got a big kick out of watching Dan's hat twirl and bounce along the Dan Ryan Expressway. Dan, surprisingly, was not amused. I instinctively grabbed my hat, thinking this to be the object of his retaliation. Dan cleverly feinted at the hat, which I secured with both hands, and then made a move for my scorecard, which was now very exposed and vulnerable. Quickly he snatched my program (I always kept score, even back then), and it was history. In a flash those pages fluttered behind us like some kind of wounded pigeon. I offered a mild protest, but my sense of justice accepted this as swift and fair treatment. Besides, the Sox lost so I really didn't care too much anyway about any kind of souvenir.

The journey continued at rush-hour speed. Word quickly spread to other seats about what just happened. Soon others got involved. A hat here and some food over there would make its way to the Dan Ryan pavement. Today I wonder about the reaction of the drivers following the bus. Try to imagine their thoughts as objects were being liberally tossed out windows. The only comparison that comes to mind is the scenes from movies when characters unload objects from a hot air balloon in flight to make travel quicker. This comparison fails, however, because our bus didn't move any faster with fewer hats and scorecards on board.

We saved the best for last. A glove. A genuine baseball glove that was as much a part of a Little Leaguer as his appendix. It's more likely that a kid on that bus would leave his house without underwear than leave without his glove wrapped around his handlebars. What kind of reaction will take place when a glove is sacrificed to the god of the Dan Ryan?

I remember this sequence well. Some kid in the back seat decided to up the ante by tossing the glove overboard. The best part was that the kid who owned the glove was not aware that it was his. His initial reaction to first hearing and seeing the glove dismissed was unabashed laughter. For a few moments we got quiet and savored the anticipation while he was roaring. Then someone broke the news to him, "Ah, Jim, ah excuse me, but I believe that glove is yours."

Like a switch, his expression changed immediately. He searched everywhere in desperate fashion, but to no avail. The level of emotion stayed the same—it just went from laughter to rage. A sublime moment. There have been only a few times in my life that I laughed so hard that I wet my pants. This was one of them.

I've used Jim to make a point when teaching morality: sometimes people don't get bothered when bad things happen, just as long as they don't happen to them.

This was the last "Little League Day" for our town at the ballpark.

The game itself hardly mattered. The Sox were playing out the string, many lengths behind the leaders. Their opponent that day, the Indians, threw someone at the Sox that was dynamite, Luis Tiant. His ageless body (I believe he was old even back then) shaked and baked and twisted and turned so much you could get dizzy just watching him, let alone trying to hit him. I suppose the most surprising news was that the Sox did manage to score two runs (one of which was earned!). The lame White Sox lineup was just what the Indians needed to break a five game losing streak.

Yet, two things out-lamed the Sox offense. One was the attendance: 4,192. This wouldn't make for a good wedding reception for some folks. The other was our seat location. We deposited our hyper-active, cotton candy-filled bodies in the right field section behind Walt Williams. From where we sat we could see why he was called "No-Neck", but it was about the only thing we could see. The batter's box might be spotted with a telescope (I guess Sox management didn't want us anywhere near the field. I can't blame them).

The game was a total mismatch. Luis Tiant, whose record after today would improve to 18-7, faced a Sox lineup that hit 39 homers as of August 10 *as a team*. With Duane Josephson as your clean-up hitter, who's followed by sluggers like Dick Kenworthy and Gail Hopkins, you might wonder how they managed 39 homers. And if the regulars should falter, big bats like Buddy Bradford, Woodie Held, and Bill Voss (with his .144 batting average) loomed large on the bench. It's no surprise that in a critical late-inning situation that Gary Peters, **a pitcher**, was called on to pinch-hit. (He drew a walk, and then another pitcher, Joe Horlen, was sent in to pinch-run. Not only did the Sox rely on their pitchers to pitch well, they also had to hit and run). With such household names as Kenworthy and Voss, it's hard to imagine how a team could be beneath the Sox in the standings. Thank God for the Senators.

GAME 24: August 13, 1968

Symptoms of an illness: "Pizza Ron turns me on," "The Cubs will percolate in '68," Bleacher Bums, Capacity crowds, and seven straight wins over the defending champs. Toward the end of summer, Cub Fever was reaching epidemic proportions.

When over 35,000 people show up at a time when crowds average 15 K, change was in the air. The good news is that the Cubs were in second place, all to themselves, with eight teams looking up to them. The bad news is that even with the remarkable success against the Cardinals, they still trailed the Redbirds by 12 games. But there was this sense that this wasn't fluky or that the Cubs were simply hot; rather, they were evolving into a pretty good team.

The ace of the Cubs pitched this game, while St. Louis' ace would go tomorrow. This was good news for me: I got to see Fergie, and better yet, I didn't get to see Gibson. I always seemed to use more lead keeping score at a Cub game; three up and three down innings were the norm on the South Side, but at Wrigley Field I got accustomed to seeing runners on base. Fergie was never going to challenge for the ERA crown, and opponents did get their hits and homers off him. Yet, in the category that matters the most, Wins, Fergie was right there. The "bend don't break" concept that applies to many football teams seemed to fit Fergie's approach to pitching. "Here it is, hit it if you can," made for a lot of strikeouts, a few homers, not very many walks, and more often than not, victories. I marveled at how such a smooth, easy-going style resulted in blazing fastballs. Fergie's style was effortless and he threw with great velocity; how many times have you seen pitchers, with contorted faces, deliver a pitch with not much on it? The problem with talent is that some may mistake effortless style with lack of effort—emotionless Fergie seemed to pitch his way into Cooperstown without breaking a sweat. I recall another great, Mike Schmidt, reporting once that his production increased when he didn't swing so hard. Interestingly, baseball takes on the "less is more" adage.

So while the Cardinals got men on base and a few runs, Fergie got the "W". (You know Fergie didn't have his "A" game when Dal Maxvill gets three hits). St. Louis was still way ahead of everyone in the standings, and looking at their lineup it's what one would expect. With the exception of Maxvill, you're staring at a bunch of tough outs. What's even worse is that they're tough outs in the clutch. Fortifying the middle of the lineup was the former Yankee, Roger Maris. I never had a chance to see Roger play before, so this was something special. With all the stories written about 1961's home run chase, I feel a type of sadness for him—a guy from the remote Dakotas in the Big Apple's spotlight. While so many people chase fame, Maris was the exception. Fame hounded him. And while I'm glad to have had the chance to see him play, I wasn't too crazy about him smacking two doubles and a single in this contest.

A tight contest it was, too, until the later innings. Santo broke the tie with a two run homer in the seventh. In the **Chicago Tribune**, Santo reports getting help with his hitting again, this time from Billy Williams. Reportedly, Billy told Santo he needed to be still—there was too much movement in his stance. It must have helped, because in the 7th Santo made the ball move about 400 feet to right center. Fittingly, he drove home his hitting consultant who had just walked before him.

Then the Cubs blew it open in the 8th frame. In the middle of it was a key 2-run single by Lee Elia off the Cubs' bench. That makes two highlights I saw in person of Elia coming up big—one with each Chicago team. Outside of his infamous tirade, I wonder how many other highlights Mr. Elia had in his Chicago tenure.

The teams combined for 25 hits, 13 by the Cubs. But with Fergie's ability to get out of jam, the final score wasn't close: 10-3 Cubs. The Bears would be proud of such a score.

POSTSEASON, 1968

The '68 World Series was an absolute delight. It lacked nothing: good pitching, good defense, good speed, good hitting, good power. It featured two cities from the Midwest, which set well with me. But in rooting for the Tigers, I was definitely in the minority. Only two other kids and our teacher (the one who thought Joe Niekro was cute) cheered for Detroit. Everyone back then seemed to have an interest in the World Series, and everyone around me seemed to be for the Cardinals. As vocal supporters for the underdog, the four of us attracted some attention.

One of the things I remember about sixth grade was that our teacher, Sister Patrice, would not allow us to play outside until the very end of the school year, much to our chagrin. Her up side was significant, however, in that she let us watch the World Series games on T.V. We're still in the era when World Series games were played during the day, be it a weekend or weekday. To watch the games on T.V. was a genuine treat; the standard procedure was smuggling in small transistor radios from our pockets into our desks. Then we'd occasionally lift up our desks (certain grades had the desktops which could be moved up and down) and quickly grab the score. (As a teacher today, I doubt that the teachers in our grade school were oblivious to our sneakiness).

My sister at home and I made a small, unfriendly wager on the Series' outcome. I had a quarter riding on the Tigers. That was big money back then. I did something then that I never did before or since—I gave up on my team and gave my sister the quarter after the Cardinals took a 3 games to 1 lead in the Series. Game 5 looked pretty grim, too, until Lou Brock was called out at home on a perfect peg from Willie Horton in left field. It was a very close play, and Brock refused to slide. His nonchalance cost the Cards dearly, as Bill Freehan recorded the putout. The whole Series turned on this play. The Tigers came back, with contributions from yet another hero, Al Kaline (I often used a model of his bat when I played in Pony League). I remember just being happy that Detroit was able to win one game at home after losing the first two.

With the scene back in St. Louis, a Tiger blow-out gave 31-game winner Denny McLain his first win. The only suspense in this game had to do with the weather. But they got it in, and I was starting to wonder if I was a bit premature about relinquishing my twenty-five cents.

Game 7 of the World Series. What could possibly be better for a group of 6th grade kids on an autumn weekday afternoon? (my brother's birthday, in fact, October 10). We were on our best behavior as our lessons were on holiday. The throbbing suspense grew with each passing goose-egg issued by Gibson and Mickey Lolich. What sometimes goes unnoticed in this epic is that Gibson pitched on three days rest; Lolich on two! Great players give great performances when it counts the most. Could Lolich, the second banana and a serviceable Chevy from Mo-town, defeat Gibson, the classy Cadillac?

The key plays in this game were misplays. In the Cardinal sixth, both Brock and Curt Flood reached, and both were promptly picked off by Lolich. Then the Tigers had two men on base in the 7th. Flood misjudged a fly ball to center off the bat of Jim Northrup. Another scene forever in my mind is this: Flood breaks in slightly, puts on the breaks, slips momentarily, and then desperately retreats. Too late. That moment was enough for the ball to sail to the wall for a triple. Game over. Yells and excitement in Sr. Patrice's classroom; no way are the Cards scoring a couple off Lolich. The last out, a pop out to the first base side, yields one last eternal memory of this dramatic Series: the embrace between Lolich and his battery-mate, Freehan. That's a lot of humanity there. Personally, for my team to come back to win after being down 3-1 in the Series and getting abused all week by my classmates was sweet indeed. One of my favorite World Series of all time.

About that quarter—I had a hard time getting it back from my sister. My dad perceived this as an opportunity to teach: a lesson to be learned here is that you should not give up because you never know what could happen. Lesson learned, pops. He's right, and to this day I can't recall ever paying a quarter to anyone before the game or the series is over. I did retrieve one quarter from my sister, and I think we called it square. That was fine with me.

PRESEASON, 1969

This summer baseball took a back seat to health. My mom seriously hurt her back late in the spring when trying to lift up the garage door (this was pre-garage door picker-uppers). From that point on, warnings about bending knees when lifting were incessant. Due to her injury, she reclined on the living room sofa for much of the summer. My brothers, sister, and I tried to do a little more around the house to pick up the obvious slack. Her rehab stint meant fewer trips to the ballpark; even I understood that there were more important things in life than baseball games.

GAME 25 April 25, 1969

Still, our family managed to squeeze in two games— one to each park. The first was totally forgettable with the Twins demolishing the Sox, 12-1. The game was not as close as the score indicates.

Comiskey Park looked weird in 1969, at least part of it did. White Sox management decided to put in artificial turf, as it was the craze at sporting cites throughout the nation. The bizarre part is that only the infield had fake grass; the outfield still had the stuff horses could eat, to quote Dick Allen. I'm not now nor then a fashion expert, and when it comes to color coordination, I've relied on significant others to advise me on colors and if certain shades blend together. So you know the colors on the field must have been hard on the eyes if I noticed it. The lime tint of the artificial turf clashed with the kelly green found in the outfield. I made the same face toward the field that my wife makes when she sees my choice of clothes as I head to work. The difference is that I can go upstairs and change; the Sox were stuck with this arrangement for an entire year. Fortunately, not too many people had to deal first-hand with this eyesore, given the attendance figures. This half-and-half experiment survived the season, and then I believe it went back to an all-natural grass surface.

The White Sox power or lack thereof implemented another physical change. Seeing that the Sox swatted very few homers during the preceding season (39 heading into mid-August), the fences were moved. Technically, new fences, about four feet in height, were installed about 10-15 feet in front of the original, no-nonsense walls. Shorter distance = more exploding scoreboards = more victories, correct? I'll use an answer I often get from my students, a definitive, "sort of." White Sox home runs jumped from 71 to 112, and the team batting average climbed from an abysmal .228 to .247. But the bottom line to a baseball fan—victories—saw an increase of exactly one, from 67 to 68. One guess why. The team ERA for the Sox ballooned from 2.75 in '68 to 4.21 in '69. Apparently the other teams liked the shortened fences, tambien.

One other quirk about the White Sox from this era— they played a number of their "home" games in a different state. Not the state of confusion or frustration, but the state of Wisconsin. How many remember the Sox playing games in Milwaukee between the time of the

Braves and the Brewers? I didn't think too much of it at the time, but had I been older and more aware, I might have seen this as the initial steps to: A) pick up a franchise in Milwaukee B) lose a franchise in Chicago or C) both "A" and "B". Even though baseball was not a$ driven a$ it i$ today, the mostly empty seats at Comiskey must have concerned Sox brass. The correct answer above is (A), as Milwaukee did inherit a baseball team when the Seattle Pilots, with their one year history, became the Milwaukee Brewers in 1970. Fortunately, the Sox did not leave.

Finally, there was the challenge of trying to follow the Sox when you weren't at the game. And by the looks of things, not too many fans were at the game. The television rights at this time went to a UHF station, which meant that the antenna and certain choice words often got a work out if you wanted to catch a few innings. The radio station was even more ludicrous. It was the type that when driving, if you turned the wrong way at a certain time, you could miss the next few pitches. You know it's bad when you can hear a game from Detroit more clearly than the one being played twenty miles away.

Enough with the stalling tactics, it's time to look at the 12-1 debacle. (Why couldn't they have played this game in Milwaukee?) This was a disaster from the get-go; one of those 60 games a team is destined to lose. I thought I might enjoy watching favorites like Oliva and Killebrew in person. What was I thinking?! I remembered closing my eyes a few times as the ball jumped yet again off the bats of Twin batters. When I reopened my eyes, it was not a pretty sight. The ball would lie between the two fences—clearing the new one but not the old one. This meant that the homer I didn't see would have just been a long fly out the previous year. DOH!

At one point in the game, my dad made the obligatory trek to the concession stand—most likely this was his way of closing his eyes. With the crowd amounting to little more than a few large families, the vendors were practically waiters. "Hi, my name is Joe, and I'll be your hot dog vendor this afternoon. Our special today is the hot dog with a side packet of mustard. Normally they go for 75 cents, but today we can offer them to you for just three dollars if you purchase four."

When my dad returned, he asked me how far over the fence did the homer(s) fly. Since I had my eyes closed, I honestly did not know. He gave me a look suggesting that I was a tad goofy, and then experienced the pain of beholding the Twinkies playing ring-around-the-bases at the White Sox expense. Since patience never was my dad's forte, he let loose with this early inning prediction, "Coming back against Chance down three runs—fat chance!" He was right. The Sox couldn't touch Dean Chance that day as the rout continued. The only fun my dad had that day was yelling at Billy Martin, **not** one of his favorites, as Martin was yelling at an umpire with his team more than comfortably ahead.

I think my dad saw that lean times were ahead for his favorite team. After this massacre, we experienced a three year sabbatical from Comiskey Park. We'd return during the '72–'73 campaigns when the grass would be just one shade of green. More importantly, the Sox fielded a competitive and entertaining team with the likes of Dick Allen, Bill Melton, and Wilbur Wood. With the bright red pinstripes at home and their powder blue uniforms on the road, this team had color and was one of my favorites. They might have played second fiddle to Charlie Finley's Athletics, but it was an enjoyable ride.

GAME 26

I've saved the best for last, and good things come to those who wait. These clichés really mean something as we attend our last game of the decade. The only Cub game I witnessed this year was a masterpiece. In fact, if you were born anytime before 1961, and if you are serious about Chicago baseball, all I have to do is give you the date, and you can take it from there: August 19, 1969.

Early in 7th grade our class was given an assignment by Mrs. Kornash. It was the kind I liked as a student, so it's also the kind I like to assign as a teacher. We were given a choice: write a composition on what we did this past summer, or write about the best moment of our life. I wrote about watching Kenny Holtzman's no-hitter in person. The teacher and classmates assumed I was going to continue and write about other things I did over the summer. No, I corrected them, I'm writing about the best moment of my life. (Note: I realize this is over-the-top and warped. I also wish to inform the readers that it's no longer my best moment, but it very well could make the top 75).

Who would have thunk it? Holtzman was good, and he proved that this day was no fluke two years later (on the day of graduating grade school, he no-hit the Reds in Cincinnati. I was waiting for some wise guys to ask me if I had a new "best moment"). But the real surprise was the opponent: the Atlanta Braves. If he threw it against one of the expansion teams, all right, nice game, but not that big a deal. But no, Holtzman allowed no hits to a lineup that featured Hank Aaron, Rico Carty, Orlando Cepeda, Felipe Alou, and Felix Milan—all very skilled hitters. This same Atlanta team would go on and win their division loaded with good teams like the Reds, Giants, and Dodgers. If you were to tell me that we were about to watch a no-hitter, I'd be willing to bet it would be the Braves' Hall-of-Famer, Phil Niekro, who would do the trick. Actually, if it wasn't for a 3-run homer into the wind by Ron Santo in the first inning, we might have been at the ballpark for a very long time. Final score: Chicago Cubs 3, Atlanta Braves 0, which means a string of 15 consecutive zeroes for the visitors and the home team after the home team's first at-bat.

Two mysterious, bordering on eerie, events marked the game. One, my sister struck out as many Braves that day as Holtzman. 27 outs and none of them strike-outs. That's pretty hard to imagine, let alone execute. You would think that with contact being made that frequently, a bleeder through the infield or a bloop in the outfield would show up somewhere. As I recall, none of the outs recorded were spectacular. Glenn Beckert robbed Alou of a hit by ranging far to his left, and one ball was hit hard but right at the centerfielder, Don Young. But it wasn't the game where you'd classify any of the plays behind Holtzman as web gems.

The other mystery was Aaron's at-bat in the seventh. Now what are the chances that arguably the greatest home run hitter of all time would ruin Holtzman's day? Well, in his third trip to the plate, Aaron hit a home run. Not the "it might be, it could be" type, but a definite, no doubt about it home run. Here's how sure I was that it was a goner: I marked on the scorecard "HR" next to Aaron's name in the 7th. I didn't close my eyes this time; I merely expected to see #44 in that patented home run trot of his, with his loose and easy style sort of gliding around the bases. I also expected to hear the crowd start to applaud Holtzman in an earnest and appreciative manner. Instead, this is what I got: Billy Williams standing with his back to us right where the indent curves back to the deeper reaches of the left field wall. I first wondered what he was doing with such an odd body pose, and then it registered: he's actually going to catch this ball! I never recall, in all the baseball games I attended anything like that. (Once at a Notre Dame football game in 1980, I swear I saw the wind die down as Harry Oliver kicked a long, game-winning field goal against Michigan). I can also confirm that I never marked down a hit of any kind in my scorecard, only to have to change it to an out (I was hoping this sort of thing would happen when I closed my eyes in the Twins' game, but no such luck). Billy later remarked that the ball was six rows back in the bleachers before the wind pushed it back. Ernie Banks got a glimpse of Aaron's face as he rounded first, and said that Henry was in utter disbelief (who better than Aaron knows when a home run is struck?) While Hammerin' Hank was stunned, Holtzman, myself, and 40,000 other people were delighted that Billy stayed with it.

The final out was also a piece of work. Aaron (who else?) was the last hope for the Braves. Holtzman fell behind in the count, but then worked it full as the final pitch was delivered (for the record, Kenny was three walks away from tossing a perfect game). Hank bounced the ball to the right of Beckert, the second baseman. For a split second my heart sank as Beckert momentarily stumbled. But he regained his balance and caught the ball. Now the words of Cub announcer Jack Brickhouse are true, clear and instructive, "Throw it kid." He does, Ernie catches, and bedlam ensues. I remember that in the scene of hysteria, Santo seemed the most hysterical—nearly jumping on Holtzman and then refusing to let go. In the stands I just sat there, stunned, not really believing what I just saw. We were deep down the right-field line in the grandstands, a place I've only sat in two or three times since, but that lucky location won't ever be forgotten. I just saw a no-hitter at the ripe age of 11. My spectating career began with a one-hitter and near perfect game; now the decade closes with the real deal.

I've sometimes wondered why fans are so self-serving and silly. They actually boast at being at memorable games, as if they deserve credit for what happened. All they did was buy the ticket, cheer a little, boo a little, and devour a Smoky Link or a Frosty Malt. Yet they talk about this game with exuberance and a pride as if they did something special. Thank God that I'm just like this.

POSTSEASON, 1969

What can be said about the collapse of the '69 Cubs and the triumph of the Amazin' Mets that hasn't been written or said many times before? I doubt if ever a second-place team got as much notoriety as the '69 Cubs. When General Patton remarked that America loves a winner, it's too bad he wasn't around for the Original Mets or the '69 Cubs. Sometimes we love losers, too.

One closing observation on the '69 affair: it just wasn't meant to be. I heard my mom use these words, not often but on occasion, and they represent a great bit of wisdom. I'd go so far to say that they're words of faith. "It just wasn't meant to be" for Aaron to homer on August 19, 1969, nor was it meant to be for the Cubs, Braves, or Orioles, who all fell to New York in September/October. I suffered tremendously as I rooted for the Braves and the Orioles to do what the Cubs couldn't, but they too came up short. The odds of defeating first a Williams & Santo, then a Cepeda & Aaron, and finally a Brooks & Frank Robinson with a Cleon Jones & Donn Clendenon are indeed amazing. But sometimes that's just the way it goes, and you can't do anything about it. It just wasn't meant to be.

NORTH-SIDE HEROES

Heroes in my first game

Hero on August 19, 1969   Hero forever

SOUTH-SIDE GOOD GUYS

Frequent tough-luck loser   Knuckleballs & birthday cake

Thrilling Save   Quite the arm

WHAT'S IN A NAME

Makes me thirsty

Makes me hungry

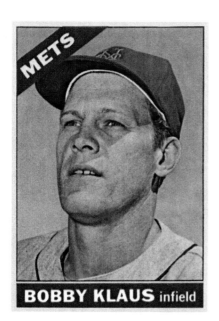

HO, HO, HO

HEART ACHES

Spoiled Larry Jackson's perfect game

Stymied the Sox on Little League Day

why trade him?

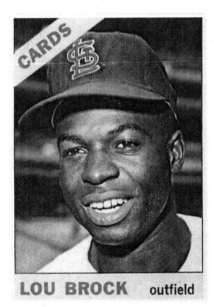

WHY TRADE HIM?

GRATITUDE

For losing the first
game I saw

For yielding Emie's 400th

For whiffing with the
bases loaded

For sharing your baseball
wisedom

EPILOGUE

Most people I know are grateful, and they express their gratitude for a variety of things: their country, their faith, their family, their friends, their health, to name those found at or near the top. I'd like to add one to that list, down near the bottom, but still on it nevertheless. That is the good fortune to be born in the Midwest where land is flat and baseball fields abundant, and to be born in Chicago, where *two* major leagues tour. How many boys growing up in the 60's can say they saw the finest teams and players from both leagues, or at least had the opportunity to do so? A New Yorker or a person from California can make that claim now, but in the 60's expansion teams from both these regions could hardly offer the history of the Cubs & White Sox. (My apologies if that smacks of arrogance, but be assured that with our track record, Chicago fans and arrogance don't mix. History, even a history of failures, offers things found only with time).

So this blessing has led to innumerable "dialogues" between both sides of town. I'd like to add to that. What follows is my attempt to compare the two identities of these organizations from the mid to late 60's, primarily. (I will sneak in things not from this era to see if you're paying attention). If you disagree with my list, great. Make up your own and I'll read it.

	Sox	Cubs
Atmosphere at games	Fights and beer	Kids and moms
Socio-economic status	Blue collar	White collar
Fan's attitude	Boy, we stink	Boy, we're great
Radio situation	What station are they on Can I pick it up?	1st in sound, service, sports
Sponsors	Friendly Bob Adams Falstaff beer	Serta beds & Old Style
Special attraction	Relief pitcher on golf carts	Pat Pieper on the P.A.
Home uniforms	Short pants?!	Cub logo's the best
Road uniforms	Drab, like all others	Wimpy two-tone hats
Most hated opponent	Cubs, then Yankees	Cardinals (Sox gaining)
Adult to kid ratio	10:1	1:80
Watering hole	McCuddy's	Cubby Bear & Murph's
What you won't see	23-22 final score	Fights
Coolest place to sit	Left field picnic area	Upper deck by home
Type of music	Hard rock	Jimmy Buffet
Big-time promotion	Disco demolitioin	Beanie babies
Fans' view of owners	#%!$%&*	Nice gum

	Sox	Cubs
When bad guys' homer	Bring in a new pitcher!	Throw it back!
Favored Opposing Player	Erine Banks	Minnie Minoso
Favorite announcer	Harry Caray	Harry Caray
Another favorite team:	Notre Dame	What other teams?
Happiest when:	Cubs lose	Ernie homers
Ideal way to win:	6-4-3 double-play	walk-off homer
Fans' hobby:	bowling	golf
Ice cream:	Vanilla w/ slight choc.	Frosty malt
Fans' attitude toward players:	Bums	all Hall-of-Famers

The author wishes to thank the fans on both sides of town. You have taught me well about baseball and about life. I'd almost wish you a City Series, but I'm fearful of the collateral damage that would result.

Regardless, since we know baseball is the greatest game, and that quality stands the test of time, we need not fear the seemingly endless issues afflicting the game. It was great long before people made such a mess, and it will be great long after these people are gone.

Made in the USA